HEAR MY STORY

WALKING WITH SURVIVORS OF SEXUAL TRAUMA

HEAR MY STORY

WALKING WITH SURVIVORS OF SEXUAL TRAUMA

EDITED BY DENISE BOSSERT

Our Sunday Visitor
Huntington, Indiana

Except where noted, the Scripture citations used in this work are taken from the *Revised Standard Version of the Bible — Second Catholic Edition* (Ignatius Edition), copyright © 1965, 1966, 2006 National Council of the Churches of Christ in the United States of America. Used by permission. All rights reserved.

26 25 24 23 22 21   1 2 3 4 5 6 7 8 9

Our Sunday Visitor Publishing Division
Our Sunday Visitor, Inc.
200 Noll Plaza
Huntington, IN 46750
www.osv.com
1-800-348-2440

ISBN: 978-1-68192-460-1 (Inventory No. T2345)
1. FAMILY & RELATIONSHIPS—Abuse—General.
2. RELIGION—Christian Ministry—Pastoral Resources.
3. RELIGION—Christianity—Catholic.

eISBN: 978-1-68192-461-8

LCCN: 2020949754

Cover and interior design: Chelsea Alt
Cover art: Adobe Stock

PRINTED IN THE UNITED STATES OF AMERICA

To all survivors of sexual trauma, may the Blessed Mother surround them in her mantle of grace and our healing Lord make all things new.

Special thanks to Jeanne Haines of Grief to Grace for her invaluable assistance in the formation of this book.

CONTENTS

EDITOR'S NOTE

You are about to read the stories of real people who have survived and triumphed over sexual trauma. Their stories will surprise and hopefully inspire you. The survivors in this book — five women, myself included, and one man — triumphed over many forms of sexual abuse, from childhood sexual trauma to rape. While our healing journeys continue, we hope that sharing our stories shows how hope can triumph in even the darkest places. Whether you are ministering to survivors of sexual trauma, or are a survivor yourself, we pray that our stories will prove that healing is possible.

Patty, Lisa, Marguerite, Jeannette, Courtney, and I are all mothers and professional women. Not all of the authors in this book, however, are women. Deacon Marty's story expresses all too well that assault of this kind is not limited to girls and women. As you will discover in these pages, one in four women and one in six men have been assaulted sexually at some point in their lives. You have either been a victim or know somebody who has. Those of us who have survived sexual trauma fight the battle with our memories, sometimes daily. We are best described as survivors. While we do not wish to be defined by our trauma, we recognize the importance of helping others overcome, and we are so thankful to be able to put this book in your hands.

Now, let's turn to you. What is your story? Are you a survivor or do you want to learn more about how you can help another heal from past trauma? Our stories and the sidebars peppered throughout this book will help you to heal or help you to become a companion in another's journey. We have prayed for you, whether you have been hurt by someone or have been called upon to accompany someone else who is hurting.

Hear our stories. Learn to walk with people just like us. Let's get on with the process of healing. May the Great Healer, Our Lord Jesus Christ, make all things new.

INTRODUCTION

The LORD is near to the brokenhearted.
Psalm 34:18

There are ghosts in this room. Not the kind that you see in movies. Not the kind that tangle with an exorcist. We push these ghosts deep into the shadows, where we believe they will remain in perpetual exile. But they don't. These are the ghosts of memories that torment in sleep and in waking hours, demanding to be brought into the light, memories that require their own kind of exorcism.

This book is the collection of good fruit from many lives touched by sexual trauma. Yes, good fruit is possible, but it only comes by way of facing down the ghosts and learning new strategies for reclaiming one's lost childhood, lost innocence, and lost peace.

From the beginning, I wanted the stories contained here to

become a book because I knew it would heal, and there are many who need to be healed. But I also wanted it to just go away. Like the ghost I exiled decades ago, I wanted it to stay below ground level where I could walk on top of it and have dominion over it. And yet — I wanted it to come into the light. To be, and not to be. That is how it is for those affected by sexual trauma. We walk among the crowds and even live among family members who do not know our pain, do not see our sickness, and have no way of knowing how to help us heal.

Perhaps you are reading this book as a survivor yourself. You are holding this book, which means you are ready to step into the Light and do your own pruning, to discover what is good after cutting away the dead branches. It will not be an easy journey. You have always known this truth; and yet, you are ready to face the memories and wrestle them, finally emerging as the victor. As you battle mixed emotions, remember that the Light is Jesus Christ. He is here, helping you to take this bit by bit, and he has already overcome the darkness. You set the parameters of how fast you go. You are in charge. Here, you will encounter people like you who can help you process your trauma. Their stories share just enough to help you to heal what must be healed. The prayers of the writers (and all who have already read this book) are constantly being lifted to the throne of grace on your behalf as you make this journey. It is solidarity. You get to open the door and let the Light grow stronger, and we pray for you. You choose which approaches work best for you. You let the writers come to you one by one and walk with you. And you find the Healer as you journey into the Light of Jesus Christ.

Perhaps more importantly, this book is for those who have never been traumatized through sexual assault. Maybe you do not have the faintest idea what it is like to have your innocence taken from you and to battle memories so dark they torment you whether asleep or awake. You want to help, and yet have no idea what to say or do. You are willing to step into another's darkness for the sole purpose of reaching for the hand of your friend and pulling her into the light of peace. Don't be afraid. You can be taught how to do just that. Moreover, you may be the only hope your loved one has for finding peace.

This is incarnational love regardless of who the victim is and who the healer is. It is incarnational in so far as Jesus Christ is the Word Incarnate. His wounds heal our wounds. He bears in his flesh the sins of all people in all ages. By his stripes, we are healed.

To the degree that we are grafted into the Body of Jesus Christ, we share in that Incarnational Mystery. Our wounds become something efficacious. We don't have to remain stuck in our trauma. We can become a venue for another's healing.

The healer bears another's crosses, tends to another's wounds, and intercedes for another. The victim becomes the healer. Do you see how very incarnational that is? The victim bears the wounds of another's sin in her body, mind, and spirit. The victim bears wounds at the hands of another, yet she can learn to bear those wounds with a forgiving heart. Jesus Christ took on flesh and bore our sin. He entered our world and walked with us. You bear the sins of another, or you have entered another's pain and walk alongside a broken soul. Jesus Christ, the Incarnate One, leads the way. Jesus Christ has shown us the way out of this trauma! Yes, you can move forward from this.

Each of the writers in this book understands the need to go at one's own pace. When we bury trauma, we cling to routine. Trusted things. Titles to hide behind. To-do lists that define days and weeks and years. But trauma doesn't hide. It doesn't decompose. It will not remain in exile. Each writer in this book has named the trauma and worked through the memories. We know ourselves better, and we know what worked and what didn't work.

You'll read my story and my scrappy journey to wholeness in a later chapter. You'll read many stories, many journeys to healing and wholeness. But we all agree: Trauma changes a person. It never ceases to be your story, but you get to define how the story ends. The only way to form it into something you can live with is to frame the experiences and memories on your terms. You shape it, until you can look at the trauma and claim it as your own thing. Not something you made, but something you have purchased at a very dear price, something you own, and something you have redefined in ways you can live with.

Trauma permits you to tell it to go, but it doesn't permit you to tell it to go away forever. It just doesn't. You heal, but the wounds never go away. One of my students once asked me why Jesus still has the wounds on his body. (I teach theology in a high school.) Even after the Resurrection, Thomas is there, reaching into the pierced side of his Lord.

I stumbled over my reply. "I suppose it is because those wounds reflect the price he paid, the work that reconciled us to his Father. It is the proof that he has triumphed over sin and death. The cross does not have the final word." The wounds give Jesus the credibility that he is who he says he is. It is proof he suffered and triumphed.

Like my trauma and the wounds of that trauma.

It never leaves.

One November, I walked into school. It had been a busy morning, and it was about all I could do to get to my classroom for a few minutes, plug in my computer, check email, and heed the call over the intercom to meet near the Learning Commons for staff prayer. It is something we do every morning. We name our petitions, someone leads the prayer, then most teachers head to their rooms. I go to the chapel. I always need just a bit more structure and grace before facing the day. In that peaceful chapel, a teacher leads the Rosary, and students wander into Our

Lord's presence as they arrive at school.

But this day took me by surprise. It laid my soul bare.

One of the teachers requested prayer for the victims of a shooting that had taken place at the Catholic Supply store in Saint Louis. We prayed. I didn't ask for details then. It wasn't the time. But as I walked from staff prayer to the chapel for the Rosary, I noticed Rachel walking close by. She had offered the petition. So, I asked, "What happened at the Catholic Supply store?"

I was ready to hear there was a shooting or a robbery. I was not ready for what I heard.

"Some guy went in the store with a gun and told the workers to take off their clothes and forced them into oral sex. One of the women refused. He shot her."

I don't know if I had trouble breathing. I don't know if I felt panic. I don't know if I wanted to cry. I don't know anything. I just know I walked toward the chapel in shock.

I went in and dipped my fingers in the holy water. I think I genuflected. I don't remember. I sat down and heard the familiar prayers. I entered into the rhythm, and my words fell off. I tried again. Again, I fell silent. That's when I knew the panic attack was coming. I looked around the chapel. I scanned the chair in front of me. My eyes traced the lines of the upholstered chair's metal frame. Up, down, over. Then my eyes darted to the floor and up the side of the wall, to the corner, along the back wall. I was shaking. I was trying to find something that would help me thwart the panic attack. I traced geometric lines with my eyes. I am used to doing this, and it usually helps.

The chair, floor, wall led me to the front of the chapel. The red candle burned. It felt like I was shaking so hard anyone looking at me could tell. I talked to Jesus in the tabernacle. There was a communion with my Lord, but it did not stop the swell of panic that refused to be turned back.

Sometimes, the Rosary is long. Interminable. That day, it

would not end. I needed it to end. I needed all of this to end. At least I had a planning period first that day. I kept telling myself I could wrestle the panic down and nobody would need to know. But the little girl in me was there, in that store. I was five. I was being told to take off my clothes. I saw the weapon. I felt the horror of wishing my feet could carry me somewhere else. I relived his demand to feed his deviancy. Repulsed, I heard and saw things from my horrific memory. I trembled as I realized dim memories could immediately become vivid again. The really crazy thing is that my trauma had made me so empathetic that I could become the victim in a story someone retells after morning prayer.

When stories come unexpectedly, when they are told in ways that are too cold, too graphic, too similar to our own, we realize that we are still healing. It is not a time to drive the memory back into the depths. It is time to say, *Okay, I need to do something about this.*

I need to seek out the solidarity of those who understand me. I need to reach for help even from someone who does not quite understand, yet loves me. In this moment, we realize that Jesus is able to enter our trauma and pain for the very same reason others feel a kind of solidarity with us. He suffered. He was the victim. He bears scars that never go away. He is right here with us.

Take a deep breath. Jesus is right here, with you now. The red candle is lit.

I'm still shaking. Why am I still shaking?

On that November morning, I didn't know what to do. I realized there is no safe place. Not even at my school, where routine is a friend and distraction is easy. Not even where I have a title that fits comfortably, and the little girl who was hurt decades ago is a faint memory, living in another house and another time.

I stood up, unable to finish the Rosary. I walked into the

principal's office and said I needed to see Cathy. The executive secretary asked if I felt okay. I looked gray, she said.

"No, I'm not okay."

It is okay to admit you are not okay on days when you are not okay.

Our principal waved for me to come in. The words spilled out, "Well, this is me in the middle of a PTSD moment. This is what it looks like."

I explained what Rachel had said and how the Catholic Supply story had triggered me. I was crying a little, and then a sob pushed up with so much anguish that it surprised me. I know it surprised Cathy. I groaned and bent over, my face in my lap. "He did it because he could. He did it because they were so innocent and vulnerable."

I was talking about them. I was talking about me — the little girl I once was.

It lasted longer than I want to admit. She asked what she could do to help. I told her there wasn't anything.

Maybe you have been there. There is nothing anyone can do. But you need to know yourself well enough to know what you can do. And I knew what I needed: I needed to go back to my classroom. I needed to throw myself into the lesson plans. Get to work. I had been here before. While it is not healthy to push the memories so far below the surface that we give them the right to pop up whenever they want to pop up, we should — we must — have tricks and techniques for cutting them down to sizes we can manage. We must tell the darkness, "You cannot have this day. You cannot have all of me. I command you, in the name of Jesus Christ, to step aside. I will deal with you later."

We must go to another person who may not have experienced what we have experienced, and we must trust enough to ask for help.

When we tremble, when we cry and it gets so ugly that others aren't sure what to do but awkwardly hand us a box of tissues, Jesus is there. Incarnational love. When we recognize another wounded person and our hearts just melt and merge, and we can't help it, Jesus is there. Incarnational love.

This solidarity is as old as the Old Covenant. In the thirty-fourth chapter of Genesis, we meet Dinah. She is a sister of the Twelve Tribes of Israel, the twelve sons of Jacob. When their sister is violated while traveling to a nearby village, nobody in Dinah's family takes her thoughts and needs into consideration. In a misguided attempt to seek justice, the brothers slaughter the perpetrator and all the men in his community. Yet Dinah's wounds are not addressed.

According to Jewish legend, Dinah is buried under a myrtle tree on Mount Arbel along the Sea of Galilee. The town of Magdala is situated in the valley between the cliff of Mount Arbel and the sea where Jesus called the apostles to come and follow. Magdala is the village where Mary Magdalene lived.

Mary Magdalene has her own story. She is branded by misunderstanding. Some say she is the woman caught in the act of adultery. Some say she is the woman possessed by demons and freed by Our Lord. Many believe she is the woman who poured out precious oil from an alabaster jar to anoint Christ prior to his Passion. We know one thing: Mary Magdalene was a woman in need of healing. We also know that she received the healing she so desperately needed, and she generously returned to the Lord out of the abundance he had given to her.

Two women separated by two thousand years — Dinah from the Old Testament and Mary Magdalene from the New. But their stories are not so different from our own. People are violated and misunderstood. Friends and family respond in broken ways. And the stories echo from the cliff and throughout the valley.

The healing Lord crosses the sea, calling us to follow. Bishops and priests, you stand *in persona Christi.* You, more than anyone else, can show incarnational love to the wounded. You were given the indelible mark of the priesthood, of holy orders, of Jesus Christ himself. You can hear confessions and offer spiritual direction. You have been given the gift of offering the anointing of the sick. You can and must help the victims to heal. You can bind up the brokenhearted. You can hold one's tortured memories in your hands, take on that wound, and help them to heal. They can encounter spiritual direction through you and leave better, stronger. Be ready to receive them, because we are living in the days of putting a voice to the pain. They will seek your help more readily than in previous generations.

Now is an acceptable time. Now is the time to lift up the brokenhearted, to free those in chains, to proclaim a year of vindication. Yes, now is a very acceptable time.

This book is meant not just for survivors of sexual assault, but for those who know and love them. Sometimes the people we count on to help us deal with trauma are stuck in their own reality and are unwilling to interrupt their lives to acknowledge that darkness and evil has happened to someone they love — and possibly at the hands of someone they know. A true companion on the journey to healing must listen to the story with empathy, believe that it really happened, grieve with the brokenhearted, and commit to participating in the journey to complete inner healing. Therefore, this book is not only for the quarter of our society who has been wounded, but it also is for anyone who is in a position to help the wounded one to heal. Believe it or not, that includes most people. Every American is either a survivor of sexual trauma or knows someone who is.

Every year 321,500 Americans are victims of rape and sexual assault. An estimated forty-two million adults are survivors of childhood sexual abuse. These survivors come from every ethnicity, family structure, gender, and socioeconomic group. The Centers for Disease Control and Prevention estimates that one in four girls and one in six boys are victims of sexual molestation. One in five women will experience rape or attempted rape.

The Department of Justice estimates that 94 percent of women who are raped experience post-traumatic stress disorder (PTSD), which affects every aspect of a survivor's life. Often, the manifestation of PTSD is the catalyst for the survivor to seek healing. This is also the moment when friends and family members look for resources that will educate them on ways to help the ones they love. This book is for you.

Bishops and priests, this book is not only for you, it is also for the ones who come to you in need of help or wishing to help someone they love. It should be readily available, perhaps even in the narthex of your parish.

Perhaps you are among the approximately 25 percent of people who have been a victim of molestation or rape, or perhaps you know someone who has been violated, and you want to understand the ramifications of their experiences so you can help your friend, sibling, child, or parishioner. Whether you have experienced sexual assault or know someone who has, this book is for you. The stories you will find here are more than stories; they contain a blueprint for healing. Each writer shares her (or his) own journey from the edge of the cliff, through the valley, and into the Lord's arms.

Let their voices become a beacon of hope.

When we are violated, something sacred is taken from us, and we fill up that void in many ways. Think about your own story. What did you do after the trauma, and how did you feel in the months and years that followed? For most of us, healing happens in slow stages.

When sexual violation occurs, the first stage is a broken

spirit. The length of time one is in this stage depends on what happens next; but after the initial shock, the heart is wounded, and this wound lasts far longer than physical wounds. If one is like Saint Maria Goretti, this stage quickly passes, and the soul surrenders to whatever comes next. But one rarely has enough grace to immediately offer the hurt up to God. For most of us, that path takes time.

The second stage is denial, bitterness, or distraction. It is possible to experience a combination of these responses during this stage. One may attempt to turn to God with the hurt, which reduces the degree of denial, bitterness, or distraction, but the wound usually does not heal quickly. Sometimes this is because those we turn to for help do not want to hear about our experiences, or they reject our story, or they blame us for what happened. In this stage, the victim usually feels lost, untethered, unprotected, empty, depressed, or angry.

As survivors of sexual assault, it's up to us to begin the journey out of denial, bitterness, and distraction. Each chapter of this book describes that journey. For some, PTSD drew them out of denial. For some, low self-esteem or difficulties in relationships compelled them to address the bitter memories. For some, professional upheaval or loss of a job or plain, old exhaustion forced them to set aside the things that once distracted them from complete healing.

While God gives us grace to turn to him at any point, this is the moment when many give up carrying or hiding the hurt. This is a crucial season for seeking the help of a spiritual director or a friend, or attending a retreat. This is the moment when a liturgical season, Bible verses, the sacraments, and adoration can bring the grace our souls seek. This is the moment when abandonment (like Saint Maria Goretti's) changes our direction and redeems us from the brink of despair. Finally, we offer every wound up to the wounds of Jesus Christ.

We learn to set boundaries, and we discover that the boundaries Jesus wants us to set are far more holy and helpful than ours ever were.

We learn to love life again, and we discover the quirkiness of our own personality and the things that bring us joy, things that reflect our unique, unrepeatable, irreplaceable, and God-created souls.

We learn to grow in holiness, and we discover that God is a perfect gentleman, never demanding, never taking, but always inviting us to a more complete and perfect union with him.

We learn how to help others, and we discover our path to sanctification. We realize that, while the violation was not part of God's perfect will, he did permit it, knowing that he would become our healer, our Savior, and our Redeemer.

Beloved, enter the journey. It will not be easy. Be courageous, because it will be better — profoundly, mysteriously, gloriously better than you can imagine.

> *Thus says the LORD … I have heard your prayer, I have seen your tears; behold, I will heal you. (2 Kings 20:5)*

LISA'S STORY

I want so much to share what has helped me heal from something that happened almost forty years ago. I do not wish to make it sound too simple or too complicated. Healing is the work of a lifetime, since we are wounded by our very nature as sinners living with other sinners, whom we hurt, and who hurt us.

As a young woman, I was an actress, and one of my mentors told our class of aspiring actors that "universality springs from specificity." She meant that our self-expression is more impactful for others when it is personal and particular, rather than second-guessed or generalized for the sake of appealing to a wider spectrum of people. It is impossible to know what will touch the heart of an audience or a reader, unless the artist trusts her own humanity to speak for itself. So, borrowing from that lesson, here I will simply share what happened and how I am healing.

I'd like to begin by sharing a very recent outpouring of thoughts, scribbled in a spiral notebook, after a scene from a movie triggered a violent emotional upheaval that I'll tell you more about later. This occurred totally unexpectedly, after my emotional life had been stable for many years. I called this entry "An exorcism":

> *The anger is terrible. The last few days, it was directed at the perp, but now it's spilling over to others, to annoyances, and people around me, and it hurts me and it hurts them. I am bleeding on them, and I can't stop the flow of this unreasonable, unaccountable rage.*
>
> *Raping someone may be the impulse of a moment, but its effects walk beside me every day of my life, like a phantom presence that can rise up suddenly with renewed venom to strike me down and violate my peace.*
>
> *My peace.*
>
> *And just like I couldn't stop him, I can't stop this rage.*
>
> *Until. I. Write. It. Down.*

I continued writing and discovered some insights. First, it was not just the trauma of the assault rearing its ugly head again with more intensity than I had ever felt before. A related source of grief was also unearthed: the sudden, clear realization that long before an alcoholic acquaintance I'll call Rick tipped the scales of my humiliation with his careless violation of my body, another man had cruelly used me and left me vulnerable to the attack.

In a rush of memories, I saw that my serious boyfriend at the time, a graphic artist I'll call Ben, never genuinely loved me. Our immature and unwise sexual relationship was probably a last desperate attempt to feel "normal." It was a hallmark of his personality that Ben could be disturbingly cold sometimes — when he wasn't being charming, creating witty collages, and playing at being in love. After we were together for ten months, he suddenly started talking about getting married, and it made him humorless and businesslike.

Ben never asked me if I even wanted to get married; it was simply part of his plan. And since he had discussed future employment possibilities with his father in preparation for our life together, I simply let him talk and lodged no protest. I felt uneasy, but I couldn't have said exactly why. So when, on the final day of our romance, my quirky boy artist phoned and asked with great seriousness to speak with me in private, I drove over immediately. He sat me at his parent's dining room table, where he recited — not a proposal, but a terse speech that amputated me from the picture: *This relationship is no longer a priority in my life …*

I can't remember the rest. In any event, he didn't say much else before suggesting we go to Friendly's for ice cream sundaes, as if we had something to celebrate. Sundaes had been our habit. We were young and silly, and heading off to Friendly's was a regular indulgence. I don't remember the drive to the restaurant or ordering my ice cream. I ate mine without enjoyment, too shocked to believe we were not still a couple and too bewildered to even object to such a meaningless and trivializing ritual. For him, the gorging that left his dish nearly clean expressed his liberation. He would never tell it to me directly, but the truth was that he couldn't wait to move to the West Coast and live openly as a gay man. I had to hear the excruciating truth later from our friends. He didn't have the guts to tell me the reason behind his cruelty. He didn't trust me to love and accept him, though I had several close gay friends. Insecure and stressed in ways I can never fully fathom, he simply terminated me and set about plotting his odyssey to freedom.

I should be grateful that Ben relocated three thousand miles away from our places and memories. His presence, while he was still in town, tormented me. I could not resist the chance to see him, and I foolishly showed up at a going-away party thrown by a friend of ours. I lurked in the shallow crowd, small-talking through the dismal hours, straining to muffle the violent struggle within me, failing to hide the pain, trying to catch his eye — while he studiously avoided mine. We left the party at the same time, and I drove behind his car, begging him out loud to pull over and *look at me*, just for a moment. When he unhurriedly turned off the main road, I forced my steering wheel to stay straight and what was left of my hope shattered into an agony of loss.

Some weeks after he left town, I got stinking drunk. Ben and I had both worked in a family restaurant, and everyone there knew us as a couple. Most of the employees were our friends; but once Ben was out of the picture, I could barely smile at anyone, let alone entertain them all, as we had done for that short ten months of frivolous togetherness. He and I had been the life of the party. But once he was gone, all the life went out of me, and something equally horrible occurred: I became instantly invisible to everyone, and the shock of that invisibility gored me from inside. One night, after work, I went off my usual script of one, maybe two beers, and started ordering Kamikaze cocktails.

The Kamikaze is made of equal parts vodka, triple sec, and lime juice. For a light drinker of the occasional draft beer, one Kamikaze is a recipe for stupefaction and idiocy. When the second drink hit me hard, I blearily inquired of the man I'm referring to as Rick, the restaurant's alcoholic bar manager, if I seemed different to him. You know, had he noticed anything? It terrified me that no one could see my anguish. How the hell could this much pain pass unnoticed?

Rick very kindly offered to talk with me in private, in the restaurant's small office, and I gladly accepted. When we were alone, I confessed the whole story of my devastation and wept aloud, while a flood of maudlin tears and snot poured hotly down my face. In sympathy, he listened a long time, and when I was puffy-eyed, soggy, and exhausted, I blew my sticky, swollen nose on a cocktail napkin. I acquiesced to his smiling offer to see me safely to my car.

We chatted our way across the late-night parking lot, and when we reached my big 1967 Buick, I unlocked the door and turned to say thanks, but his arms went around me, and he leaned in to kiss me. I wasn't afraid. I was just repulsed at the thought of anyone kissing the sticky mess of my face. In that moment, I uttered the first of perhaps a dozen, very definite *NO*s. When he started to back off and open my car door for me, I was relieved, and I slipped in behind the wheel, wondering whether I was okay to drive. But he pushed in next to me and recommenced kissing and caressing.

I told him to knock it off and repeated my refusal. But with a strength that made my protests irrelevant, he pushed me down onto the wide front seat, thus making his point with great clarity, and somewhere between sitting up and tumbling backward, my state of consciousness shifted profoundly. I fell into a place of darkest despair, where grief, betrayal, alcohol, and this sudden horror fused and expanded into a psychological shockwave. I remember this bleak thought rolling over me in slow motion: *Well ... if he doesn't care about me ... then I don't care, either.* And some part of my mind broke loose and floated away.

What followed only affected me dimly, as from a great distance. I could feel almost nothing and became limp and compliant. When he finished and sat up cheerily behind the steering wheel, getting his pants in order and chattering happily as though we'd just shared a romantic interlude, I got up, too. I pulled my clothes together and sat staring straight ahead, silent and numb. I don't remember what he talked about, just that he was chipper and enthusiastic.

The moment he finally stepped out of the car and the door clicked shut, my left arm shot straight out, as if of its own accord, and slammed down the manual door lock. It is a small comfort that some part of my mind was still alert and able to spring into self-protective action, however belatedly. I swiftly checked the three remaining doors, as I watched him stroll back to the restaurant.

When he was out of sight, I slid behind the wheel and started my car. I remember thinking how sober I felt. The world was strangely calm and silent. I did not go to a hospital or call the police. I drove home and told no one. In fact, in what would become a chronic state of confusion about the assault, my own reaction, and the fact of my drunken condition, it took me ten years to call what had happened a rape. It would take me another twenty-seven years to begin to grieve.

For many years, mostly ignoring what had happened was the best I could do. I never sought professional help, and I no longer felt safe, emotionally or otherwise. And while I have a typical creative temperament that is quick to feel and almost a quick to express, I couldn't quite get what salesmen call "buyin" from my listeners, so I rarely spoke of it. I know now that I failed at describing the experience adequately to people close to me because I was not confident I understood it myself. I was still confused, and my confusion confused them. And when they didn't react as I thought they should — with shock, sympathy,and a desire to comfort me — I felt abandoned and unloved.

LISTENING TO SOMEONE'S STORY

Take the sharing of someone's story as a special and important moment. Most people never tell anyone. They find it too difficult. It makes them feel vulnerable and fearful. They have too much shame and self-blame. For a survivor, telling their story is one of the most difficult things they will ever do. It's excruciating. They are wondering how you will judge them They fear that you will see them as the dirty and broken person that they believe themselves to be. They are telling their story, forcing themselves to relive the experience, only because telling their story has become less painful than the idea of keeping it all inside. It has finally become more excruciating to keep it inside than to push through all those fears and share.

Our memories are fragmented, sometimes confusing. Sometimes, the survivor's brain has a hard time making sense of what happened. The shame makes it difficult to share and screams to them to keep it hidden. They push through. In sharing their story, there is a small hope that they will not be blamed and will somehow be loved and accepted. The greatest fear is that the listener will not believe them or will question their actions and confirm that the survivor is at fault, enforcing their feelings of shame and being unlovable.

While sharing their story, their body can have physical reactions. It might be feeling the same sensations that they experienced during the trauma. They might feel pain or distress. Their heart may start racing. Their blood pressure increases. They may have headaches or pain in areas where they were injured. They may dissociate.

The brain will cut itself off from the body as a way to cope and not feel all those feelings again. It is very common for people to dissociate or black out when they are being abused. Our brains don't know what to do with that experience, because we were not created to be abused.

I've had the privilege of being the first point of contact and the first person for many people to share their story of sexual abuse. This is due to my profession, but also because of the simple fact that I ask. I open the door for them to talk.

Have you ever experienced sexual abuse or sexual trauma? There are some therapists who don't ask this often enough. It's a very uncomfortable question to ask, even for therapists. I have found it to be an essential question. Asking that question has allowed clients the ability and freedom to share. I have discovered that many more people than you would think have experienced sexual trauma.

In a therapy session, I am an impartial party. I often hear: *I haven't told anyone because they would see me differently or I haven't told anyone because they would be angry and want me to act.* Sometimes I hear, *Others wouldn't believe me or I'm afraid others will judge me.*

The problem was that I had a very specific picture of what an innocent victim looked like, and it didn't jibe with my experience. It chills me to write this, but to me, a victim worthy of love and sympathy had to carry physical scars, as a testament to both the crime and to her righteous efforts at self-defense. I had no physical scars because I had given in to my attacker. So the scars that wounded me most deeply were buried deep in my psyche, where they festered and planted a seed of shame so corrosive that it gradually bled my life of all its beauty.

WHY DON'T SURVIVORS SHARE THEIR STORIES?

Survivors are often afraid of judgment. They are already judging themselves. They fear others will start to see them the way they see themselves. They believe they are dirty, shameful, sinful. They feel so much shame. They believe that the act of sharing will cause the listener to view them in this dark light and make them feel even more ashamed.

Survivors are afraid of not being believed. This is a valid fear, because it happens all too often. Many listeners don't believe because they don't want to live in a world where things like this happen.

It's important that the listener avoids asking questions that can create a feeling of not believing. Avoid questions like Did it really happen like that? or Did they really do that?

Remember that your job is not to fix them (hopefully, you feel a little relief at this). Remember that you are not a therapist. Your goal is to be a grounding, accepting, and empathetic person for them. Your job is to walk with them and direct them to a place where they can have even more support and help. Your job is to show up and be present.

Simply listen. Reflect on what they say. Use their words, not your own. Restate how they described the situation to you. Avoid telling them how to think or feel. It's often tempting to try to show the survivor how awful the abuser(s) were and that they shouldn't feel guilt or blame themselves. Don't! It's extremely difficult for survivors to not blame themselves. They have ingrained this self-blame in their mind. You are merely pointing out yet another thing they can't do and will fail at.

Grant them the belief that they are inherently good. There is usually a sense of deep-seated shame. They feel that they are dirty, bad, and sinful. They believe that that is why such terrible things have happened to them. Your goal is to let them know that they aren't a horrible person. Let them know that they are good. Simply state, "You are so good." It will be difficult for them to take this in or to recognize that you said it, but it's a seed you start to plant.

One of my favorite summaries of what stance to take when listening is summarized by Bessel Van Der Kolk:

I gradually came to realize that the only thing that makes it possible to do the work of healing trauma is awe at the dedication to survival that enabled my patients to endure their abuse and then to endure the dark nights of the soul that inevitably occur on the road to recovery.

It takes great bravery and strength for them to share their story with you. They are fighting every instinct telling them to flee and forget everything. Their body, their memories, their triggers, and their current struggles won't let them.

Grounding. You are here to ground the survivor. You are here to be grounded with them. Together, you can hold to the present reality.

Grounding is being in the present moment. When telling an abuse story, survivors can be taken to the past. They can get lost in past memories. They may no longer realize where they actually are, or who they are with, or sense their current surroundings. They may not even be able to feel their own feet. "Grounded means that you can feel your butt in the chair, see the light coming through the window, feel the tension in your calves, and the hear the wind stirring the tree outside" (Kolk, 2014).

This is important for you to realize. In your encounter with survivors, they may not be in the present with you. The past hijacks their brain. You can sometimes tell when they are not present by noticing where they are looking. If their eyes are stuck in one place, their brain is likely back in the past. They may look like they are daydreaming.

You can help someone become grounded with subtle reminders of the present. Simply state, I am here with you.

Use all the senses. Ask them to name things in the physical room with you. Ask them to name things they see, hear, smell, touch, or taste in the present. Bring them back to the present by bringing their senses to the present. Use a soft, calm voice.

If someone asks to talk to you, suggest taking a walk. Walking and talking helps to promote healing. Really! It's about movement. In the trauma, they were trapped and couldn't do anything. They felt helpless. Symptoms of trauma can perpetuate this feeling of helplessness, leaving them in the constant state of being helpless. Walking or other movement helps the survivor regain a sense of control. The ability to take a small action helps the brain remember that they can do something, and they are no longer trapped and helpless. Walk with the survivor. Toss a ball around. Allow them to interact with water.

In 1992, I hit rock bottom and fell headlong into a deep conversion. I have written about it in more detail in my book, *True Radiance: Finding Grace in the Second Half of Life*, but I will share some of the relevant pieces here.

I was an actress in New York City and already married to my good husband (of over thirty years, now!), but in those days, infertility made each month a cycle of expectation and devastation that led to feelings of hopelessness. As an actress, I'd seen and experienced plenty of what has been exposed in the #MeToo movement. People in power could be predatory, and my once fearless creative life spiraled into debilitating fears that resulted in missed opportunities and stunted creativity. As my career stalled, my relationships were strained to the breaking point, and

I came to believe that God was just another cold, dominating male who had utterly abandoned me. I prayed with my fist in the air, hating him for creating me but failing to love me. I hated him more every day because my own self-hatred was so ferocious.

In an attempt to break away from everyone and everything, I undertook a weekend-long trip out of state that plunged me even deeper into crisis. Yet, on that journey, through a series of "coincidental" encounters with women (Jesus wisely avoided sending men, at this point), Our Lady drew me to the Holy Rosary, which brought me back to Jesus, as well as the Catholic Church and the transforming powers unleashed through a renewed sacramental life.

Conversion flooded my soul with graces. Daily Eucharist and frequent confessions healed many wounds that I didn't even know I had. The graces of this super-powered combination of sacraments, along with a daily Rosary, brought light and life and beauty flooding back into my soul. It became easier and easier to see and embrace beauty in myself, in the world, and in other people. I learned to seek forgiveness and to cultivate an attitude of mercy. In time, I learned to at least try to let go of everything and give it all to God, every day.

Many years into this healing process, our family moved from Brooklyn out to the suburbs of Long Island, and I started driving regularly again. Within the first year, my car was struck twice by distracted motorists. The first was a doped-up construction worker on his way to a job site. He plowed into the back of my car, giving me a terrible case of whiplash. Several months later, an elderly driver in a massive SUV blew through a stop sign and hit the right front side of my car, smashing it to bits. From that moment on, I drove everywhere in a state of increasing tension, fearing the third impact was just around every corner. It was like having a loaded gun pointed at my head.

One day I started crying and couldn't stop, so I reached out to a therapist for an evaluation. I was suffering from post-traumatic stress, the therapist said, but she didn't think it was only the car accidents that had caused the condition. "Every trauma," she explained, "triggers every other trauma from the past." The latest car accident had simply pushed my system to a breaking point, and it was necessary to go into the past and find the original source of this overwhelming sense of danger. She suggested medication for short-term relief, which I refused. My daughter was little, and I had to drive her everywhere. I wasn't willing to risk impairing my reaction times or judgment behind the wheel. So we talked and sifted through my history, which pretty quickly unearthed the assault.

She introduced me to a therapy called EMDR (Eye Movement Desensitization and Reprocessing), which involves alternately stimulating the two sides of the brain in a totally non-invasive way. It's a process that was discovered accidentally by a therapist named Francine Shapiro, and it has been one of the most effective ways of decreasing the intensity of emotional distress associated with traumatic memories for all sorts of people: assault victims, veterans, those who have lost loved ones through violence, and so on. For some reason, an alternating stimulus helps the mind to integrate emotions into the present, so that the memories no longer plunge the patient into the raw trauma locked in their unconscious experiences of the past.

After only two sessions of EMDR, I was able to face conflicts with loved ones without breaking down in tears or becoming angry. I could simply state my case calmly, with the expectation that I could handle whatever followed. This new sense of emotional equilibrium caused others to treat me with more respect, which enhanced my own growing self-respect. I can't say enough about what this one, brief experience did to help me to feel comfortable in my own skin again. I don't mean that all of my fears left me — I don't know if they ever will — but they shrank in size and became manageable. And my tendency to be hyper-vigilant in my relationships, waiting for emotional dangers and criticisms, also declined. I was able to interpret people's intentions more charitably, to live with less anger, and to experience a greater sense of control in my life.

I recently heard a Catholic speaker say, in reference to the anti-Christian culture we live in, that "they buried us, but they didn't know we were seeds!" When I searched for the origin of the saying, I found that the second-century Christian writer, Tertullian, famously stated, "The blood of the martyrs is the seed of the Church." The sacrifice of the martyrs gives life to the Church, and their relics can help believers to open more deeply to God's life-giving grace. So, it follows that our own wounds can be access points for this same growth, expansion, benefit, and fruit-bearing abundance. Jesus is Lord of Life, the inseparable Second Person of the Most Holy Trinity. God himself was stripped and abused, and the gates of heaven opened as a result.

Our Lord promised that we would perform even greater works than his (see Jn 14:12), so it is, in a sense, a spiritual *superpower* to have suffered. The saints rejoiced in their sufferings because the graces were so amazing. We who have been deeply wounded have much to offer God for the salvation of souls, in union with the cross of Jesus Christ. The fertile ground of the survivor's heart is a place where great abundance can spring forth and benefit the Church and even the whole world. I'm not saying I'm glad I was hurt, and I am grieved that you who are reading this may also have been hurt. However, I rejoice in the regeneration and restoration provided by the love of God.

In the Book of Joel (2:25), God makes an extraordinary promise to the children of Israel who suffered exile and famine due to the sins of the people: "I will restore to you the years which the swarming locust has eaten," he declares. He vows to not only provide healing but also restoration and blessing that will dwarf their losses.

Countless times, I have prayed for the grace to forgive the man who attacked me, to forgive my "debtor," desiring sincerely to save his poor, broken soul. It motivates me to think of snatching a soul away from the devil. Saint Thérèse of Lisieux prayed as a young girl for the salvation of a condemned murderer and won him for heaven, even as he stood on the scaffold! I like to think my little prayers and the intention of forgiveness, however imperfect, combine in a powerful one-two punch that shakes things up. God's power is made perfect in weakness, and I am proud of my dependence on him (2 Cor 12:9).

For many years after the EMDR therapy, my emotional life remained stable, while my spiritual life continued to flourish. It took a series of grace-filled but stressful life changes to move me to the next level of healing. We sold our home and bought another that needed renovations, in order to bring my mother-in-law to live with us. I've noticed that God moves powerfully during times of transition. I suppose that when I am being forced to stretch and accommodate new challenges, I am probably open to the Holy Spirit in a special way.

When Denise Bossert approached me about contributing to this book, I was touched and very happy to say yes. In public, I have alluded to the assault as part of my conversion story, and many women have shared their own pain with me, often in tears, after my talks. The hugs and knowing looks we share bring our hearts into instant intimacy. I thank God for yet another way he can bring beauty from devastation. It took me several months to begin writing, however. Thinking and praying about such a traumatic experience began to stir something dormant that I was fearful of acknowledging. Each time I approached my computer with the intention of making a start, I drew back in fear.

One night, my husband and I were watching a movie, a murder mystery. In a flashback scene, it became apparent that a young woman was about to be raped. Normally, my husband simply fast-forwards through such scenes, for my sake, but this time I jumped up and left the room, standing in the kitchen with my hands over my ears, like a terrified child. I could still hear the ominous soundtrack, so I bolted upstairs into my darkened bedroom and fled to the window farthest from the stairwell. I stared into the night, taking solace from the silhouetted trees undulating beautifully in the wind, while tears slipped down my cheeks in a steady stream.

Such things aren't ideal for a healthy functioning mind. Be mindful of what is being shown, talked about, and discussed. Another thing to consider is that someone else sharing their abuse story can be triggering for other survivors. If someone is sharing their story to others, have resources available for all those present.

Soon, my husband came to me and enfolded me in his strong arms. Within that embrace, I immediately felt profoundly safe, and yet a shriek burst from me and crescendoed into high-pitched, wracking sobs that were completely beyond my control. In a frenzy of release, my body shook all over, and I doubled over. The strength drained out of my legs, and I collapsed to the carpet, my husband gently easing me down. On all fours, I wailed helplessly, clawing at the rug under my hands, my eyes wild, as if I were searching for something in the dark. I had the terrifying thought, *I don't know if I'm coming back from this.* I was descending into the past, and I did not know the way back. I was grateful for my husband's gentle touch and soothing voice, throughout.

After several minutes, the keening wails lost intensity and wound down into sobbing, which gradually calmed and quieted. For weeks afterward, I was emotionally brittle and prone to sudden tears. I was also aware of a white-hot rage boiling up inside, as I entertained vivid fantasies of hurting the man who had hurt me. This was totally new to me, but as alien as this state of being was,

I sensed that I was in a new place of potential healing and that I needed professional help to put it into perspective. I made an appointment with a therapist recommended by a friend.

The therapy session itself was actually pretty dreadful. The therapist kept checking status updates on her phone while I told my story! Yet, she said one thing that really helped: "Sometimes it takes years before we allow ourselves to grieve." As soon as I heard it, everything fell into place, and I was able to simply grieve. My emotions no longer frightened me, and I was able to process the feelings more smoothly. For that, I am so grateful to that distracted lady. God bless her!

Not long after that session, my daughter came home for a visit from college and said, "You've never looked happier!" and it was true. Just letting myself be angry and grieve was the next layer peeling off, helping me to feel even more comfortable in my own skin, to be less threatened by life and more confident that I can live with what's left of my scars.

Daily life is also a source of healing. I hear God most clearly in my vocation, so it is in serving my family, sacrificing for them, praying for them, that I draw closest to God and hear his guidance in my soul. It's not always easy to live out my vocation in an attitude of self-gift — Saint Teresa of Calcutta says that "if we love our vocation, we will be tempted" — and serving others is not always what I would rather be doing (let's be honest). However, I experience a deep certainty of God's presence when I die to self in small ways throughout the day, and it gets easier the more I practice an awareness of the needs of others. The result is an abiding joy and increased affection among us, which brings trust, gratitude, and humility into our relationships.

Conversely, when I find myself slipping — all too often — into selfishness, I experience desolation almost immediately. My world becomes small and colorless, until I repent and push myself to get moving again toward God and away from self-indulgence, ugly thoughts, judgment, criticism, and the desire to punish others. Frequent trips to the confessional are invaluable at these times.

Holy Mass is my almost daily food. Without this intimate communion with Jesus, I tend to lose focus and lose heart. Confession is the way I meet Jesus to clear out the gunk in my soul and let more of his divine healing reach into my life, often opening up relationships and perceptions in surprising ways. The Rosary is my lifeline and daily discipline. The Novena of Abandonment has helped me to give my life increasingly to Jesus. The Divine Mercy Chaplet is a source of restorative graces. Offering my ordinary work for various prayer intentions and in praise of God gives everything in my life more meaning and purpose. I avoid rushing too quickly into my own plans and try always to stay open to God's.

A few years ago, I took a self-defense class and amazed myself with the unbridled passion and enjoyment of my kicks and punches. I fell in love with martial arts and launched into an intensive study that lasted only a few months, until I injured a bone in my ankle; yet, the practice gave me new confidence in my own physical capabilities.

Things are not perfect, of course. I still compulsively check the locks on my home and my car, and anxious thoughts sometimes assail me unexpectedly. But I know to turn from disastrous imaginings, since they do not come from God. I return my gaze to Jesus, knowing that as long as I fix my eyes on him, I will not sink into the waves (Mt 14:29). He upholds me in love.

BEING SENSITIVE TO TRIGGERS

Triggers show up unannounced and unexpected. They cause extreme anxiety and panic attacks. They even cause anxiety when they aren't actively present; the survivor can be in constant fear that they might show up any place at any time. Sometimes this results in a state of constant fear that lasts for many, many years.

When a trigger is activated, it hijacks the brain. The ability to think rationally is completely cut off. This is sudden. The survivor may not even be able to realize the change.

Abuse creates hypervigilant watchtowers in the brain. These towers stand ready to sound the alarm at a moment's notice. They constantly look for signs of danger. These signs can hide anywhere: people, places, things, times, weather, facial expressions, physical motions, a phrase, a seemingly normal word. Almost anything has the potential to trigger a faulty alarm system in the brain. This leads to emotional blowups or a total shutdown and retreat. The instinctual fight, flight, or freeze takes over.

When the listener is faced with a trigger situation, it's important not to judge or criticize any of these reactions. Never say, "You shouldn't respond in that way." This creates more feelings of brokenness and emphasizes that the survivor's internal wiring is faulty. (Usually they already know this about themselves, and it's a source of self-loathing.) Instead, simply acknowledge any reaction that may not make sense to you. While the alarm is blaring, there is no reasoning with the alarm. No insight can be gained.

Be sensitive to triggers. Be on the lookout for subjects or areas the survivor seems to be trying to avoid.

For instance, it's okay to want to avoid watching movies. Certain scenes in movies and television and other visual media often display content that can trigger survivors of abuse. Scenes of sexual, physical, and emotional violence are not normal to see, no matter how many times they are portrayed. Our brains don't know what to do with that information. This confusion can get stuck in our nervous systems, revealing itself as anxiety in our everyday lives. Everyone should be cautious in exposing themselves to this kind of content.

Some of the greatest and most liberating mysteries of our human existence have been boiled down to aphorisms and trite maxims that roll off our tongues and fail to move us. So, it may seem glib to state that powerful graces are found at the foot of the cross of Jesus Christ. Yet, it is true that the way of the cross is the way to true happiness, that Jesus is that way, and that he calls us to have life and to have it in an abundance that can only come through him. Jesus, the stripped and abused victim who knows our pain, has showed the way for us to grasp and live out the redemptive power of suffering offered in love to God. He provides his mysterious example for us to cling to; and, unexpectedly perhaps, he then shows us the way to living in glory.

Jesus promised that when we put our faith in him, we will do greater things than even he has done (Jn 14:12). It is so hard for us to believe that, but it's the reality that is present to us in every moment of every day, sometimes out of reach because of our own false narratives. We can make the mistake of living in the past, processing everything through our pain, which becomes our safe haven from disappointment and danger. The pain of the past, we may unknowingly believe, is familiar territory and therefore our identity and destiny, while the possibility of freedom seems too far ahead of us, too elusive to inspire our faith. But Jesus said to so many people, "Your faith has made you well," so I cling to faith, as my joy increases over time.

PRAYER

Dear Wounded Savior and Lord of Life,

You have proved that no matter what is taken from me, you can restore me.

In my daily calling, tending my soul's garden through mundane and hidden acts of service and self-gift, you infuse my soul with light and speak to me most clearly.

Through sacramental healing, you bring radiant warmth to my dark places, and you dwell even in the darkness itself: mysterious, holy beyond imagining, loving me through pathways unseen and unfelt.

Some days I see clearly the abundance and generosity of your presence. Other days are harder, but you bring great fruit from those days, if I lean into you and say very simply, even without conviction, out of the poverty of a weak faith, "Jesus, I trust in you."

Thank you, Jesus, for taking what is ugly, bitter, and lifeless in me and flooding it with beauty.

I am glad to be alive. I am proud to be yours. I am happy.

Amen.

OVER-SPIRITUALIZING

Too often, survivors bear further wounds of not feeling like a good Christian. They believe they are sinful. They believe they are not good enough. They believe they are unlovable by God and the Church. Sometimes, they believe that they are abandoned by God.

They've been told that they just need to pray more. They just need to have more trust in God. They need to forgive more. They've been told that doing these things will cause the memories to go away, and then they will feel better. They've tried. And failed. These demands have created an even greater sense of hopelessness, rejection, and isolation. As much as they desire to trust more, to forgive and to forget, the trauma won't let them. This often results in the thought that *I must not be good enough. I must have deserved it.*

Trying to over-spiritualize the solution, even with the best of intentions, often leads to the worst of results. Don't let yourself go down this road. Instead, just listen. Let them know you are there to help them find the help that they need. This is especially true in the confessional. They need counseling and support. They do not need to be told where they are failing. If you don't know what to say or do, that's okay. You don't have to. Refer them to a qualified therapist.

It's also important to realize that your response should not be merely spiritual. They need more than prayers. They need boundaries, safety, a sense of predictability, acceptance, and love.

Survivors are often referred to priests for counseling. Talking with a priest is very helpful in most situations, but not all. Seeking sexual abuse counseling from any person not trained in this area can be very dangerous and often exacerbate the issues. A priest's training doesn't include all the tools needed to respond to all the needs of the survivor. Please refer them to a qualified mental health professional.

DENISE'S STORY

It was a time when children overheard young people and adults asking one another if they knew the singer John Denver and his hit "Country Roads." Flower power and paisley dominated the fashion world, and long, straight hair was in.

We lived on a corner where two country roads met in rural Iowa. That is where I heard the young men talking to my dad about the song and the album that he just had to get. Dad pastored their little Wesleyan church with its adjacent cemetery. Here, boys in their late teens caught garter snakes in the gully one year and married pretty girls a year or two later. The window of time between teen antics and matrimony was very small. I suppose that was a lot to take in for any young man trying to maneuver the transition.

I remember him being right there in the middle of the older boys. He looked at those older guys with longing, too young to be one of them and too old to not care.

It may be strange to begin with him. It may be even stranger to describe him as a "he," rather than how he seemed to me, the kid in kindergarten. But that is what I have had to do to understand things that cannot be understood and to process things that trigger emotional tailspins.

He was a young man. He wanted what was not his. He knew there were ways of getting what he wanted.

I pray he outgrew all of that, but for decades, I only thought about what he did to me and not about what might have been a pattern of behavior that followed him into adulthood. I was only a little child trying to forget. The mind has ways of doing that, but Protestantism and the lack of the Sacrament of Reconciliation make forgiveness and discerning things like culpability, power, and deviancy really dicey. Yet, there I was, alone in the journey to forget.

For years I kept busy so I wouldn't think about what happened. Today, I'm a Catholic writer, speaker, and educator — one of those unlikely converts to our beautiful faith. The conversion led to speaking and countless venues for telling my stories, all but this one. Then I had a year that was quiet. My youngest headed off to college. My three grown children started families of their own. I wasn't working, and life was too quiet. The buried past is often exhumed in silence.

The introspection began a couple of years earlier with a commitment to regular confession and spiritual direction. My priest and I covered a lot of ground, just not that ground. One can be physically busy, so as not to remember. One can be spiritually busy, addressing every weakness and wound except the ones that are buried in the depths of the soul. I had some experiences that were buried so deep that nobody would have guessed that I had ever been molested.

I saw a meme on social media recently that said, "You had a great childhood if … " and there was a picture of a leather and metal roller skate. It is odd how images can take us back to events in childhood — only this wasn't an idyllic memory. It was an image from my worst moment in childhood. Suddenly, I was back there.

A roller skate, discarded in the middle of the concrete basement floor. It was the day my sister and I played at Tori's house. Her older brother was babysitting us. My sister and Tori ran upstairs and left me with him.

He lured me under the stairwell of that unfinished basement full of random toys and a bed and stuff that gets stored downstairs and relegated to the place beneath. That's how basements in other people's homes feel when you are five: the place beneath. The place where used things go, where stuff gets hidden so visitors can't see it. The concrete has a smell. The junk that's down there has a smell. Even the wood that frames the stairs to the main floor has a smell. The senses are on hyper-alert, but especially the eyes. The eyes see everything. And they remember.

He stood facing me, his back to an exterior wall, my back to the framework that held up the stairs above our heads. He reached into his pocket and pulled out something. "Do it, or I will use this."

I can still see what he held in his upturned palm — a pocket knife. Every boy's best friend. But to this boy it was power and it was control, and I was so little. It's the kind of terror that wraps you up suddenly and tightly. You want to flee, but your feet feel stuck. Only your arm is free, your hand, the one that could reach out and touch the weapon but never wrestle it away. You feel your smallness.

What he told me to do made no sense to me. Who would do that? Who would *demand* that? Cold, metallic fear filled me. I imagined doing what he said — for just a second. The revulsion almost made me physically ill. I have told young people in their Safe Touch classes to do whatever it takes to get away safely. I have told them to say they have to throw up. And when faced with situations like this, you actually do feel like you might throw up. The Safe Touch kids don't know my story, but they laugh at my suggestions to just say I'm going to throw up. It gets results, and they know it. Teachers back away and say, "Go, go to the nurses." And parents usher them into the bathroom *tout suite*.

But I was too afraid to tell the young man anything. I thought the only thing to say that would keep me safe was "okay." Everything waited for my yes, but everything in me said no. I could never do that. I was old enough to know what that part of the body did every few hours. I guess my mind could not deal with what was happening, because I can't remember what happened next. Everything goes blank. It cuts out. It ends with no resolution.

The next thing I remember is being upstairs. My sister and Tori were in her parents' bedroom, talking. I remember looking at them and wishing they had stayed with me. They might have protected me. The two of them together could have done that. But they didn't. I kept it all to myself. Now, as an adult thinking back on it, I am quite sure they knew what he wanted. While I thought he liked me in some confusing way, I realize now that he just wanted power and control over someone who could fulfill a deviant desire. Any of the three of us could have fit the profile. I began to wonder why they were so quick to run upstairs together. Were they trying to get away from the very experience they left me to face?

I have also wondered about our parents. Where were they? We were, after all, still fives and sixes, and yet they left three little girls with a young teen male. Most young men want nothing to do with girls that young, and it was not an era when anyone talked about "the predators you might know." People were only beginning to talk about the stranger-predator. We were also caught in the time when children were supposed to acquiesce to any adult demand and, above all, to be respectful.

It was difficult to know how to respond to this young man in the in-between stage, our male babysitter. But in just a few minutes, he had taught me to be afraid and suspicious. In just a few minutes, he had changed my life.

Every pocket knife, for the rest of my life, would bring it all back. Every single one.

Weeks or months later, I remember being with him again, at our house this time. We were walking between my house and the church. My father was a pastor, which made me a preacher's kid. The space between the house and the church was all the same to me. It went together, like a rectory and the parish church. There was a party going on at our house. Not the kind of party where people drink, but a party where evangelical Protestant Christians got together and played board games and ate chips and dip. The young man persuaded me to go into the church, where we sat on the landing inside the back door. He must have realized how much he scared me the first time, because this time he was nice, totally different. The change in approach threw me off guard. I don't know why I followed him into the Sunday school classroom, but I did. He had threatened me with a knife the last time we were alone; yet there I was, following him across the yard, up the back steps, into the empty church.

Maybe I wanted to change our last encounter. I didn't want to be afraid of him. He was being so kind. Maybe it would make the bad feelings go away if I could replace that memory with a new, lighter and kinder memory. Maybe I had been taught to be compliant when someone much older told you to do something. Or maybe I was curious. He was older and paying attention to me. Maybe that felt good.

In the last few years, as I have processed that early trauma, I have wondered whether I was part of his learning curve. I have considered the possibility that he learned from me what approach would work best. I have hated myself for going with him that second time. I see that girl, following along like a puppy, crossing the yard between the parsonage and the church where two country roads meet.

Even so, I followed him. I remember a little more about this day. There was still some fear — and unwarranted feelings of guilt. He didn't demand something as crazy this time. This was something I did every time I got in a bathtub or changed my clothes, except there would be someone watching me. Still, something was wrong with his demand, and it filled me with shame to comply. I was glad nobody found us there. Years later, I wondered what would have happened if we had been found. I wondered whether adults would have blamed both of us. I still wonder.

Shortly after that incident, my father took another parish, and we moved. I had a born-again conversion, which was a rite of passage as an evangelical Protestant. I asked Jesus to come into my heart and to forgive me. The experiences with the young man were begging to be addressed. I felt relief. Now I could give what happened to Jesus, because it felt like I had sinned, and he would forgive me and forget that it had ever happened. God could do that: forgive and forget. We didn't have confession to a priest, so there was no one to say, "My dear little one, this is not your sin." But it felt like I had been forgiven for the sin I believed was mine. That gave me strength.

The boy visited again because his parents and my parents were best friends. He pulled me into our attic. I went, but this time, when he made a demand, I said, "I don't do that anymore. I am born again. And God doesn't want me to do that."

I don't know why he respected my answer this time, when he clearly had no respect for little girls. But he let me go. I didn't tell anyone what had happened to me even then. I forgave him, and in time, I came to terms with the fact that he had been a mixed-up teenager with nobody to talk to about taboo subjects like sexual sin.

Later, when I came to recognize the treasure of the Sacrament of Reconciliation, I wished we could have had the peace and wisdom of the confessional at a time we both needed it for different reasons. As a Catholic convert, I also had a new view of what happened. I could see these moments of trauma and add in the supernatural reality that Jesus was there when I was threatened. He stood beside me, gave my feet flight. Archangel Michael was there, especially the third time when I invoked the name of Jesus and the boy shrunk back, withdrawing his demand. And that first time, the most traumatic of all, when the boy had a knife and his demand was absolutely unthinkable for a girl so young and innocent, Saint Maria Goretti was with me, praying and praying and praying.

I had an army fighting for me. The trauma would not have the last word. But the battle had only just begun.

BROKEN BOUNDARIES

Survivors of abuse have had their personal boundaries severely violated. This breaking of trust is rarely acknowledged. Their boundaries are not respected, sometimes over and over and over again. This makes it difficult for survivors to learn that it is okay to have boundaries or even that boundaries exist. When they try to form boundaries, they don't know what healthy or appropriate boundaries need to look like.

Healthy relationship boundaries have two dimensions: connectedness (those boundaries that help one be a part of a relationship) and separateness (those boundaries that help one be independent) (Heitritter & Vought, 2006). Having had one or both of these violated makes it incredibly difficult for survivors to tell the difference between what situations and people are safe and unsafe.

The survivor's image of healthy relationship boundaries is distorted. Their connectedness boundaries desire constant contact, reassurance, and responsiveness. Anxiety increases when these needs are not being met or responded to. Their separateness boundaries can be distorted to the point where the very thought of relying on someone feels dangerous. Their walls don't want them to be vulnerable. The very act of communicating or spending time with others causes primal fear. Survivors sometimes find themselves bouncing between these two extremes, desiring intimate contact one moment and being deathly afraid of contact the next.

By the time I was in fifth grade, I began to act out on the trauma. It is not uncommon for a child who has been sexualized at an early age to exhibit signs of the experience. One summer, while visiting cousins in South Dakota, we walked over to a vacant house on their ranch and explored old clothes in the closets and jumped on the bed with musty-smelling blankets. We pretended to be grown up and living in this vacant house. Something reminded me of the musty smell of a basement and the parent-less time in a house. We were all girls of about the same age, so I felt a freedom, like I had escaped the age of being a little victim.

It was the era of Sonny and Cher. I pretended to be Cher with her clothing and lack of style inhibitions. I took off my clothes and bounced around with a Hollywood confidence. It was stupid and spontaneous and rooted in the experience of molestation in ways I still don't fully grasp. And then it was over, and I felt dumb and confused by my actions.

Someone told my mother.

I spent the next day in a small bedroom in my aunt's house, all alone. My mother quoted a verse from Scripture, "Be sure, your sins will find you out." And she left me there to talk to God about what I had done. To this day, the tears burn behind my eyes when I type out the story. I swallow hard at this point. I've never said the words out loud. What I did was stupid. What came after the moment in the old house was horrifyingly embarrassing and filled with shame and confusion. That afternoon stings. Even now, it stings.

It is compounded by other family situations and stories that are not mine to tell. This is important to mention in passing: Every offense and every violation affects those who have been traumatized; they create triggers and a host of feelings and memories. Stories intersect because the victims are relatives or friends, and always, it seems as though there are many lost opportunities, many moments of failed heroism. We need to change that. We need to become vigilant, empathetic people who protect and defend at any cost.

The parents of that era and faith heritage groomed children to be good, respectful, and almost asexual until the wedding night. This meant that children were ill-equipped to respond to sexual violation and even sexual desire. We kept it buried and prayed that God would forgive whatever-that-was under the stairwell, in the Sunday school classroom, in a vacant house in South Dakota. We got on with the business of growing up. Years later, my parents went back to participate in a church anniversary celebration. The now-grown-up predator approached my father and said he felt he needed to apologize for what he had done.

I sat beside my father's bed as he retold this story of their conversation a few years after it happened. Dad was very ill by this time, but I think he might have put the pieces together. Dad told me, "I asked him why he felt the need to confess to me. He said he always respected me. And I wondered what he had done to make him feel like he needed to tell me about it."

"What did he say?" I asked my father. I was ready to talk about the molestation if Dad knew, but the story would break his heart if he didn't know. He was too fragile now to talk about such things. But if he already knew, that would change everything. The news wouldn't come as a shock, and maybe we could speak of it for once.

Dad shook his head and continued. "He looked at me a minute, kind of quiet, and then said he had been drinking a lot and been to Cedar Rapids doing things a married man shouldn't do. I guess he wanted to get it off his chest." Dad looked at me then.

I lowered my eyes and nodded my head. So, he couldn't bring himself to tell my dad what was really haunting him. When he realized that Dad didn't know the truth, he pulled back his confession.

Dad sat quietly for a moment. Then he said, "I still don't know why he needed to ask for my forgiveness." The ache in my heart was so painful. I wanted to spare my father the hurt. He had made it this far through life without finding out what a kid in his church had done to his little girl. I was angry at the boy and the man he had become. The mix of emotions was almost more than I could control.

I felt so much love for my father at that moment. I honestly believe he had figured it out. Dad was amazing like that. He had empathy and a special kind of discernment. What he didn't see in his little girl and when his daughter was a boy-crazy teen, well, I think it all finally made sense to him, but neither of us could say the words out loud. As always, he just looked at me with total love. None of it changed how much he loved me, but there was a sadness in his eyes. God had given me a father who loved unconditionally. Dad died a few weeks later.

My mother never remarried. Every now and then, she talks on the phone with an old friend who lost his wife shortly after Dad died. He is the predator's father. It is strange how the triggers never stop. I find it so odd that I am glad she has someone to talk to and, at the same time, find it terribly ironic that it is his dad. It's like seeing a bruise on your arm and deliberately pushing on it to see if it hurts. It always hurts. What made you think it wouldn't? You just frown a bit before moving on to something that isn't shrouded in really old memories.

The journey wasn't over. Power. Control. Feeling trapped. Feeling exposed. It began to affect other areas of my life. Delayed-onset PTSD led to social anxiety. The adoration chapel where we gathered for daily Mass had the same architectural design as the little church where I had been abused as a child. I stopped going to daily Mass.

I still gave talks and wrote because the writer or speaker can be in charge of the parameters. I could let people in, but they couldn't get too close. I researched workshops and retreats. There weren't any near me at that time. I went to spiritual direction, and my priest was the first person to prompt me to pick up past trauma and begin to heal.

My priest said I could probably keep going as I was. I had managed to do that for decades, and I had gotten quite good at it. There would be healing in the eternal realm, he said; but, he wanted me to know, there was healing possible right now if I wanted it. I did.

The counseling was invaluable. I learned how to place boundaries and make sure others observed them. I received the Sacrament of the Anointing of the Sick. I hoped for an immediate healing, but it didn't happen like that. Yet I did begin to heal.

When I started writing about sexual assault, my family

didn't understand. My mother and sister didn't think what had happened to me was as traumatic as I was making it out to be. I wrote anyway. I wrote because *I had to write*. It was fitful at first. Cathartic. A rant here. A raw emotion there. And then it became something more, something better — a sanctification of the wound.

The voices who joined mine came from everywhere. Even in the Church, there are many who have been violated by family, friends, acquaintances, and strangers. We are not immune to this violation just because we are faithful followers.

These are wounds that never go away. They change how we think. They change how we move through life. But I am learning that he who is our suffering Lord, our wounded Christ, says, *Offer these things up to me. They will become an efficacious prayer.*

The sorrowful mysteries of the Rosary and the Stations of the Cross have become powerful prayers for me. Sometimes, I just need to take a walk in the backyard. Sometimes, I get up in the middle of the night and sit in the living room — pray and doze, doze and pray. I sit with the daily readings, and they minister to me. I plant seeds and put them in my garden window. They usually die before I get them in the ground, but I need the process even if I don't have a green thumb. There is something about soil and seeds — a little green pushing through the black, those first leaves that move toward the sunlight outside the window.

I travel frequently to the Holy Land. It comforts me to walk where Jesus walked. The Sea of Galilee is healing balm for my soul. I sometimes climb Mount Arbel along the Sea of Galilee. At the end of my first climb, I panicked when I realized that the very last part of the trek was straight up a rock wall with metal grips drilled into the cliff. I managed to haul this middle-aged body up the side of a cliff. That was the year I came home and began the journey of healing from sexual trauma. I had no idea that climbing Mount Arbel had anything to do with the healing process. I did not know that victory over metal handgrips and toeholds on the side of a mountain would crush the grip of the image of metal roller skates in my head.

I reread the story of Dinah in Genesis 34. Dinah was raped, and nobody handled her violation correctly. Her post-rape journey is filled with one tragedy after another. I wrote to my friend who lives near Jerusalem and asked her whether Dinah was buried at the Cave of Machpelah near Jerusalem like the other matriarchs and patriarchs.

"According to Jewish tradition, she's buried on Mount Arbel," my friend texted back.

No way, I thought. This is deep grace. Dinah is crying out for all to be healed. Dinah, the sister of the Twelve Tribes, is interceding. It is time for the Church to be a venue for healing.

I have spent a lifetime giving myself away emotionally, professionally, and sometimes physically. One can barely make sense of the stops and starts in relationships and employment when the inability to set boundaries dogged me at every step. At first, there is a temptation to shout at everyone to back off, even when another's foot approaches my perceived boundary but does not cross it. I am not fluent in this new language of setting personal limits. I put heated accents in places that require a delicate touch.

Recently, I had a nightmare. The sex trafficker had a pocket knife in his hand. I pulled away and ran through city block after city block in the dark. I have dreams like that once a week. Sometimes more. I wake up and give it to Jesus. We wrestle with it together, and then I get on with the day. Jesus Christ calms the waters of our emotions and sends a special grace so that we might know how to live the paradox: freely giving yourself for Christ's sake, but realizing that the enemy prowls around seeking those he might devour.

I largely overlooked another helper God has given me — my guardian angel — until recently. I invited him to walk with me and set boundaries on my right and on my left. I walk with Mary's maternal mantle wrapped around me. And my patron saint intercedes from heaven's throne. I am glad for this great kingdom that I cannot see.

It is heaven's healing balm, and the jar never runs dry.

PRAYER

Lord,

I know that you have given me free will to choose my path: healing now or healing later. I choose healing now. I realize that healing begins with giving you my wounds. I offer them up now for all those who have been hurt.

Let my feet find the journey to the cross; let me experience the joy of your resurrection and help me to know the great miracle of my redemption.

Let the fiat of Mother Mary and the perfect miracle of the Incarnation transform my memories into something new. Let me become as Saint Maria Goretti, an intercessor and healer for those who come after me.

Turn the oil of sorrow into the oil of gladness. And let my light shine in the darkness.

Amen.

HOW CAN I HELP A SURVIVOR DISCOVER HEALTHY BOUNDARIES?

It's critically important to be aware of the survivor's possible struggles with boundaries. You know that those boundaries have had the potential to be damaged or even broken, but this doesn't have to be purely a guessing game on your part. You can build trust and comfort levels by asking for permission for anything involving boundaries. Let the survivor know that they are in control of those boundaries. *Is it okay for me to sit here next to you? Would you prefer I sat over here instead?*

Remember that tendencies you may have to comfort someone with physical touch may not be comforting. Ask first. While your intention may be to give a comforting hug, realize that a hug can often be invasive and anxiety-provoking. Ask first. *Is it okay for me to give you a hug?*

Any actions that disrupt the survivor's needed space can take their attention away from telling their story. Such actions can set the act of healing back.

You must build trust, expectations, and safety.

- Set appropriate times, spaces, and durations to meet up, talk, and connect.
- Be consistent and reliable.
- Let them have choices in where and how to meet up. Allow them to create a sense of agency and control.
- Allow space for them to say no.
- Respect that space.
- Allow their "no" to mean "no."

Remember that they may not know what appropriate boundaries look like. It's important to demonstrate and communicate appropriate boundaries. This is especially true for leaders in the Church.

- Establish appropriate times and durations to talk.
- Establish appropriate places to meet.

This point can't be stressed enough. In my time working with the Church, this is something I often had to teach and reinforce to Church leaders. Forgetting to establish these appropriate times and places can cause issues and confusion. It can even damage the survivor's boundaries even more. Survivors may not know what to expect from social situations; that knowledge gap is likely replaced with a sense of danger. Time and place boundaries need to be the first thing that is set and communicated. Take the time to communicate these expectations. Take extreme caution to make sure you meet the expected boundaries.

COURTNEY'S STORY

It's strange what we remember from kindergarten, because early memories are like fleeting scenes from a movie. We are in the scenes, but we don't remember memorizing any lines or having a director block the scene. We didn't realize that there was a camera rolling or that the scenes would be permanently housed in our memories, for good or bad. We just lived, and the camera caught everything.

I remember when I was in kindergarten. I was lying on my parents' bed, and my mother was sitting on the edge of the bed talking to me. I don't know what the surrounding conversation was or what led up to this sentence, but I remember my mother telling me that I was her biggest surprise. That can be taken several ways, I suppose, depending on how you look at it, but I think at the time she thought I would take it as if I were a wonderful gift, unexpectedly dropped off by the stork on her front step or a late birthday package.

Yet even then, at only five, I felt like that sentence had dark undertones, and I was uncomfortable. I knew that other things hid behind the words, and I knew they were things I wouldn't understand, and I wouldn't want to know. I knew that surprises weren't always surrounded by curlicue ribbons and helium balloons. Surprises sometimes meant feeling uncomfortable, frozen, confused. Surprises sometimes meant somebody else was manipulating the scene, the stage, the lighting, the words, the whole thing. And the surprise ending isn't always one we expect — or even want.

I knew my mom wanted me now. But I also knew that something else hid behind the glistening eyes, the smiling lips, the cryptic words.

In retrospect, I know now exactly why it had dark undertones and how my barely-out-of-toddlerhood brain knew that it took a mommy and a daddy to make a baby. I even knew some of how it happened, although no one had explained it to me. So when I became a teenager, I would joke with a small hint of sadness that I was "mommy's little mistake." Realistically, a part of me did feel this way, especially during my times of rebellion when I would see the look of defeat and disappointment on her face and interpret the meaning: "Why was I so careless as to have a third child when I was perfectly fine with two?"

More recently, I've come to find out that those words were darker than I ever could have imagined. I wasn't a happy surprise or an accident or even a "mommy's mistake" as I had joked. I was conceived in rape. Daddy forced himself on mommy. Nine months later, I was born.

I always wonder in what order my earliest memories happened. The cutting and splicing in the editing room of my brain didn't preserve the chronology very well, even if it did a splendid job of preserving memories I'd rather forget. The earliest memories are dark, as if whatever room I was in had terrible lighting.

The memories I have of my mom's conversation in her bedroom are clear, bright. The memories I have of making "milkshakes" with my brother and using cups of sand and sticks for straws seem like they happened on a cloudy day. I still remember the sand between my teeth from truly putting the stick in my mouth, fully committing to our childhood play. The memory I have of standing in a crib and my sister opening the door to the bedroom is dark, like nighttime, just like the memory of the room with the wood-paneled walls. As if it had no windows, only a closed door and hardly any light.

The memories of that room are three-second clips here, two seconds there, then the ending. There was no need for the rest. That's all I need to know about what happened in that room when I was a small child.

When I was a little girl, Dad was Dad. I didn't know any other dad, so that was it. Dad had done things that I hated, but what else was there? Didn't all dads do that? When I was twelve, I began putting those clips together, and it was like a slow realization of what had actually happened. The movie reel waited for me to figure it out. It just kept playing in my head until I understood. It waited for me.

My brain didn't want it to be true. I wanted to reason it out to be something other than what it was. But I was old enough that I couldn't deny that all dads did *not* do *that.*

At fifteen, I finally convinced myself to speak to my mother about it for the first time. I was surprised when my mom believed me. For years I had debated saying anything because of the horrible thought that I might be called a liar or told I was being dramatic or that I made the whole thing up. After all, I had just spent many years trying unsuccessfully to convince myself that I had made it all up, but the truth was the truth no matter how much I didn't want to believe it, no matter how sick it made me feel.

Mom believed me, and that brought its own kind of healing. I never questioned exactly what made her believe that a man who had been a preacher, a youth leader, someone whom so many looked upon fondly, could do the things I was telling her he did.

My mother told me more details about how I was conceived. My father had not only molested me, but he also had forced himself on my mother. We agreed that he was messed up for doing that, but we didn't discuss or label it further at the time.

Over the years, I learned some things. I learned that sex without consent is rape no matter what the surrounding circumstances are. I learned that rape doesn't have to accompany kidnapping or being tossed into a van, and it didn't have to be 2:00 a.m. in a dangerous park. I learned that I was conceived because my dad forced himself on my mom, and that is rape.

Now the interesting thing about it all is this: My mom struggles with more anger toward my father for what he did to me, but I am far more angry at my father for what he did to her.

I feel that everything that has happened in my life, every mess I have tangled myself up in, and every standard bad decision with a daddy-issue causation has a flipside of victory, because I have simply survived them all. By the grace of God, I am not a drug addict. I am not suicidal. I generally enjoy life, despite the craziness that followed each catastrophe. I feel alive. My mom believed me and that was good enough to keep me from falling too far or too deep.

But my mom carries clearer memories. She raised tangible proof that something horrible happened to her, and she chose to love me in spite of how my heart came to beat. And when everybody knew what had happened to her, nobody reacted the way they should have. She was the one who was considered questionable and dramatic. This is the precise fear I had as a twelve-year-old, the reason I didn't speak about it until I was fifteen. The last thing I wanted was to not be taken seriously. I watched as that happened to my mother, and it is heartbreaking.

What about me? Well, I am awake at 1:30 on a Thursday morning, writing. It is one of the ways I process pain. I put the words in places where they won't be found, or maybe they will. I inherited that method of exorcising past hurts and joys from my mother and her father. I think it is a path to healing.

My mother and my grandfather have also been instrumental in my healing. Sometimes people hurt us. Sometimes, other people help us to heal. My grandfather — Mom's dad — was like that. I was hardly tall enough to see over his desk, but mesmerized by his penchant for collecting knickknacks and collectibles and candy dispensers. He dealt in serendipitous humor and few words, but the words were spot on. The gift of words, like humor, goes out, and the wise one (and the needy one) finds it.

Grandpa was like that. His discipline was just a look and never a hand, and that was enough. His love was just a look and never a question, and that was enough. Books on tape on the way to work. Hankerings for ice cream after every meal, never too many times a week. It feels like he still smiles at me, even though he is mostly a collection of memories in a box in Mom's basement. I see reminders of him, and I know that he intercedes.

Those who pass away in Christ are like that. They are in a place of humility because they are hidden, yet more present than ever before. They don't hold grudges for being retired to a box of memorabilia. They wait, not for us to turn to them, but for us to turn to God with their help. They want the little knickknacks to be a path to remembering that they can and do intercede.

I miss Grandpa, but I'm glad he missed the mistakes I made. In the scope of eternity, he didn't miss a thing, but he was spared the desolation that one feels when someone we love falls. And I fell — hard. Again and again. He interceded, as did many others.

As I transitioned from teen to adult, I retained some of that awkward little girl who didn't fit in anywhere in particular. I might have been bullied, had I not had such a sharp, defensive tongue. Church was the only stable thing in my life that I allowed myself to hold on to, a place where I learned that God loved me and created me, and I was not an accident. I was meant to be here on this earth despite the circumstances of my conception.

My mother is all-in Catholic. When I was a homeschooled seventeen-year-old with hardly a social life, my mom started to become my friend. I would sit on her bed and listen to her talk about the Faith.

Her stories and theories were fascinating. I was introduced to deeper aspects of faith, like the communion of the saints. She told me the Catholic Church was the very first church to exist. I had never looked into why Catholics had a pope or how that came to be, or even that it was in the Bible that Jesus had appointed Peter as the first pope, saying, "Now I say to you that you are Peter (which means 'rock'), and upon this rock I will build my church, and all the powers of hell will not conquer it" (Mt 16:18, NLT 2007). My mother explained to me the purpose of the statues of the saints and the purpose of bowing before entering a pew to sit in church, why we touch the holy water and make the Sign of the Cross before Mass every week, why holy Communion was to be received weekly, and most importantly, what holy Communion actually was. She broke down every sacrament in detail.

The Eucharist was the game-changer. When she told me that the bread and the wine were not a mere representation of the body and blood of Christ, but that in fact it *was* the holy body and sacred blood of Jesus himself, which had broken and spilled for each one of our sins, I knew this was true. "I *am* the living bread that came down from heaven. If anyone eats of this bread, he will live forever. And the bread that I will give for the life of the world is my flesh" (Jn 6:51, ESV).

When she asked me how I felt about this teaching, I was happy to tell her it sat soundly with me. "Then you were meant for the Catholic Church!" she responded. At that moment, I wanted to say that she wasn't in charge of editing my movie reel. I was. The next scene would not be my conversion. She was wrong. Instead of grounding myself in the Catholic Church, I was out to prove that I was not a follower — I was my own person with my own mind, and I might choose my grandpa's faith or no faith at all. I moved away from home at the age of eighteen. I was an adult, ready to be in charge of myself. I was now attracted to what had been taboo. I can't say I became an out-of-control drug addict or self-destructive lost girl, but I dabbled in enough distractions to keep me from any particular path.

Eventually, I became pregnant with my first son. When he was born, I wanted to fix everything immediately for him. At the time, my vision of what "right" looked like did not match what was. My extremely rocky and periodically abusive relationship with my son's father did not fit the picture of a happy family. It felt like I was fighting the world on a daily basis to make sure everything appeared to be as good as possible. When I became pregnant with my second son very shortly after my first was born, I knew that making things appear to be right might have been good enough for me, but it was not good enough for my children.

I knew moving back home was the best thing to do, but I was also intensely worried that I would have to fall back into being the follower and the good girl, something I had actively rejected for many years. I missed God, whom I had actively rejected for a long time. Even in my time before the boys were born, I outwardly refused religion. But inwardly I longed for it. I yearned for the stability and safety I had known in church when I was a kid, and I even prayed that I would find that goodness in other things.

I still wasn't ready to become Catholic, and I didn't like the idea of submitting to papal authority. I think it also had something to do with daddy issues, and with my grief over the loss of my grandfather. And with my own maladjustment toward anyone telling me to do anything.

One day while driving my car with my boys in their car seats, I found myself crying and didn't know why. I stopped at a stop sign, and I heard God's voice for the first time in a long time. The only thing he said to me was, "Courtney, stop fighting." And I knew exactly what he meant.

It was a long road filled with stops and starts, but I finally submitted to grace.

CRYING TOGETHER

When hearing of someone's experience, the listener may be moved to cry. It's important that these tears say, *These are for you. These are not for me. These tears are here in this moment. They hear you. They share your pain. They are because of your pain. They are not for my pain. They are not because of my experiences. They are for you and you alone.*

Don't allow yourself to become emotional or emotionally reactive. A common way this manifests itself is when the listener becomes upset and angry and starts listing all the things that need to be done in order to bring justice. Survivors tend to be sensitive to burdening anyone else with their pain. They don't want to make someone else upset or feel bad for them. They don't want to live with the memories and pain, so why would they want anyone else to glimpse what they have experienced? In fact, the listener's emotional response can cause the survivor to feel obligated to take on the role of the comforter.

Big emotions can be scary. The survivor may have spent a lifetime training themselves to be numb, burying emotions. They've made themselves believe that emotions are shameful. Causing someone else to feel big emotions is even more shameful. The listener's big emotions may cause the survivor to become confused, anxious, or even shut down.

This doesn't mean that the listener must keep their emotions secret. It simply means the listener must be aware of these emotions and keep them in control.

Let the emotion simply be. Let it be okay to be vulnerable. Let it be okay to cry. You aren't there to solve the emotion. You aren't there to make it go away. Let it be.

Fix-it mode is off limits. Diving into the list of tasks and actions that can solve things may cause the survivor to shut down, close up, and not trust you with their vulnerabilities. In the moment of sharing, the survivor just needs space to share, the feeling of love and acceptance, and the freedom from pressure to *solve*. The mere idea of taking steps toward a solution can feel insurmountable. The only time it's okay to try to "fix" things is when the survivor specifically asks for help or expresses a need.

When a father not only abdicates his place as a true father, but leaves scars of molestation on his daughter's childhood, she takes hold of her life and nobody can loosen that grip. But the conundrum is this: You still need God.

In fact, you need him more than anyone ever needed him.

I needed the God who had always loved me, who loved me even when I was suffering from one of the worst kinds of trauma a little girl can endure. I needed my sons to know God. I wanted them to have a spiritual guide that would clarify what was expected of them as Christian men. When my children saw my unsettled nature, my own shortcomings, they needed to know that even I had a grounding, a rock that was greater — far greater — than I am.

Motherhood had become my reason to heal and grow in faith.

Our faith teaches us many things. My own mother is quick to remind me that this faith affirms that we are unrepeatable, irreplaceable, unique, and gifted. That is an important message for every child, but it is an especially important message for children conceived in rape.

I have come to embrace my uniqueness. It is a path to ongoing restoration. I think it is important for every survivor to embrace those things that make them feel alive and special. Let those who love flowers buy flowers. Let those who love a good manicure get one. Let those who need a canine or feline companion have one. Let those who love a good book have shelves and shelves of them. Let those who like to bake try out one recipe after another. Let those who need to take long walks or hike up a mountain do it.

Let all that has breath praise the Lord in myriad ways. We are his masterpieces, created for good works in Christ Jesus. Let us live in them. Let us live and move and have our being in our Creator, not the brokenness that once defined us.

PRAYER

Lord,

You tell me I am wonderfully made (Ps 139:14). You tell me that you knew me before you formed me (Jer 1:5). I belong. This belonging is something that I cannot see, and something I sometimes do not feel. But you have placed your sign upon me and claimed me as your own.

I am not claimed as a thing to be used, not as someone who does not have freedom to say yes or no, to go here rather than there. I am claimed by a Redeemer who gave everything so that I could live in the Light of Christ. Here, there is true freedom.

I choose Christ, for he first chose me and called me to produce good fruit (Jn 15:16). I know it is true. We are each one wonderfully made.

Amen.

A WALKING STORY

(This is a real story told in the first person. Names and details are removed to protect identities.)

I received a call from school personnel who didn't know what to do. They had been contacted by a person whose therapist suggested she physically visit the places she had been molested. She had asked the school if it was okay to come in and walk around, visiting each room where events had occurred years ago. The school didn't know what to do with the situation and was hesitant to grant the request. They called to consult me on what to do. I told them to go ahead and let me know the date and time so I could be present.

When she arrived, I met with the survivor and introduced myself, explaining why I was there. My position as part of the diocese had an unexpected impact. I really had no idea my presence would make such an impact. With tears streaming down her face, she was in shock when she realized that the Church did care about her, that it cared about what she went through, and that she didn't have to be alone in her healing journey.

This taught me that our simple presence can be extremely meaningful.

I walked with her up and down the hallways as she told me her story. She wanted to walk into the rooms alone. As we finished visiting the various locations and returned to the front office, I could tell things had changed. Her body attitude, demeanor, and body posture had changed. She had tears streaming down her face. She asked for a hug and told me, "It's gone. I left the pain in the rooms."

I felt truly blessed to be a witness to this healing moment. This is where I learned the meaning of walking with someone. I had done nothing out of the ordinary. I hadn't used any mind-blowing therapeutic techniques. I simply was there with her. I didn't ask for details of what happened; I let her lead. The experience was about her and what she needed.

I just walked with her.

When you are serving, be with whomever you are serving in the moment. Look at them. Let them know you will be there when needed.

We can't begin to understand what Jesus was going through while carrying the cross, but we can walk with him. We can witness him, take notice, and be moved. We can be Simon of Cyrene.

PATTY'S STORY

"Where sin increased, grace abounded all the more" (Rom 5:20).

There was a time I didn't understand Saint Paul's spiritual riddle. I didn't understand how grace could ever arise where sin had staked its claim. Today, this verse is like a banner over my life. Today, grace abounds.

The anger, pain, and resentment I once carried left no room for the light of Christ. I was consumed by distrust and bitterness, a stranger to peace. I felt unworthy of love. In a moment of darkness, I begged the Lord to help me. *Jesus Christ, mend the broken pieces of my life.*

Broken. Until about six years ago, that word defined me. It described how I thought, how I acted and reacted, and how I summed up my life. It began when I was only a child and slowly became a way of life as I suffered injustices at the hands of individuals who selfishly destroyed my innocence.

My parents were migrant workers and decided to live part of the year in Idaho with family and friends in order to secure stable farm work. Some people think children don't have the capacity to remember what happens to them when they are young; and yet here I am, forty years later, still haunted by the memories of my traumatic childhood. I was around five years old when everything started. Both of my parents had to work, so they needed someone to watch me. The wife of one of the ranch hands stayed home while her husband and their older children worked. On the surface, the arrangement must have seemed perfect.

The husband always reeked of beer and sweat, a smell that still paralyzes me and makes me nauseated. They were an older couple with teenage kids, and it was obvious that the husband believed he had the right to dictate orders to everyone. He came home for lunch every day, and his wife began asking me to take him his lunch to his truck. I didn't realize he had told her to send me. I didn't realize that she knew what would happen when I went.

I just wanted to give him his lunch and go back to playing, but he became angry as I turned to walk away and demanded that I get in the truck. He leaned over and opened the door. I just stood there, hesitating. The truck was old and dirty, and there were empty beer cans in brown paper bags all over the floor. It smelled terrible. Sweat, beer, oil, and dirt. It was a stench that lingered even after I got out of the truck, even after the truck was part of a past memory.

He began asking me how much I loved my parents and how I would feel if something happened to them. He had no intentions of listening to my answers and quickly began to make threats. He said that I had to be good and that I had to do as he said, or he would tell his wife and she would hit me with a wet branch that she kept in a 25-pound bucket of Armour Lard. I had seen her hit her own kids with that branch and immediately remembered the pain on their faces as she struck them.

He asked me to come closer, and when I didn't, he reached out and grabbed me, planting me next to him. My heart was pounding so hard I was sure someone would hear it and come find me. I closed my eyes, but fear compelled me to look. He was undoing his belt and the zipper to his pants. Again, I closed my eyes and clenched my fist tightly as I felt him forcing me to open my hand. I was scared and kept doing the opposite of what he demanded. He eventually grew angry and frustrated and his threats became more detailed, more explicit. He said that he was going to hurt my parents if I didn't obey, and that if anything bad happened to them it would be my fault and there would be no one left to take care of me.

He was enraged, and I believed he meant every word he said.

The loneliness I felt when he began touching me was as terrifying as the man who caused it. I felt like I had been abandoned in that truck, like I might never again know what it was like to be safe and to know the security of protective love.

I began to dread lunchtime. As soon as the wife began cooking, I would think of places to hide. My heart would race, and I would feel sick to my stomach because I knew what was coming. The sound of his truck driving up the road terrified me. One day I hid in the barn behind an old tractor. My heart was beating so hard that I could feel it pounding in my ears. I could barely breathe from the fear, but I continued to hide because I didn't want to be in that truck alone with him again.

I felt so dirty and scared, and going home was no better. I was afraid that someone would see the fear in my face, and they would find out how disgusting I was. Other times I feared that he would think that I told someone, and he would kill my parents, and it would be my fault.

I finally stepped out of the barn when I knew he was long gone. I needed to use the bathroom. She was waiting. She spanked me, and I felt the burning and stinging for hours. She made me kneel in a corner on the porch, and I eventually fell asleep, exhausted from having cried so much. She was furious when she found me asleep, and she spanked me again.

One day, she purposely pushed me into the electrical barbed-wire fence. She laughed as I tried to recover from the jolt. Another time she made me kneel on splinters. I wonder if I had marks. Were there any signs that I was suffering physical, mental, emotional, psychological, and sexual abuse?

My courageous days of hiding became fewer and fewer as they managed to break my spirit. He continued to take all my firsts. He had robbed me of my first touch, my first caress, my first kiss, and she always made sure that I did what he said.

He began taking me to the barn, and his abuse became more invasive and painful. By this point, I remember crying when my parents dropped me off, and she would convince them that I always stopped crying as soon as they left. My parents believed her.

His threats became more elaborate and descriptive.

Over the years, as farming seasons went by, he grew confident that no one would find out what he did to me everyday. I looked forward to the winter months when we went back to Texas and was happy to see the first palm tree because I knew it meant we were home and I was safe, even if it was for just a few months. I dreaded when it was time to go back and the packing and preparation began. Over time, I began to feel numb. I wasn't in a perpetual state of terror. The abuse had become routine, and I no longer cared what happened to me.

The abused often have triggers. A smell. A place. A thing. Those who violate leave the wounded with triggers. Stale beer. Switches for whipping. Barbed wire. Old pickup trucks. Ramshackle barns.

My memory pieces together the things that happened that

last time. Fighting. Demands. Hot sauce on his hands and now on me. Burning. My head feeling like it was going to explode. Screaming. Being pulled to the bathroom. Running water. A need for water. Compliance as the clothes came off. A searching for the water, a wiping of tears, and then the hot sauce burning my eyes, too.

He laughed as I cried and bumped into him, trying to feel my way toward the flow of water. Then I felt a sharp, piercing pain between my legs that ran up my back. It felt as if my entire body was being torn to shreds, and I desperately tried to focus through stinging eyes. As I looked down, I saw that I was standing in blood-tinged water, and I hoped it meant that I would be dead soon. It was the first and only time I saw fear in his eyes.

I don't have any memory of what happened after that. God permitted me to black out or forget what happened next. I only remember waking up because my parents were there to pick me up. The woman told my mom I had fallen outside and cried myself to sleep. The man stopped coming home for lunch after that, and the following season my dad was hired by a different rancher. I never went back there again.

Years later I told my parents about the abuse after seeing the man at a family funeral. I felt a surge of anger as old feelings surfaced. I had hoped that telling another person might help me find closure, but I was told I should be ashamed of myself for making such horrible accusations against people who had loved me and raised me like their own. I learned to keep the secrets and the wounds to myself.

Wounds change us. Even when abuse stops, we compensate for the trauma. My short temper, my inability to trust, and my anger toward men were things I struggled with daily. I had a hard time establishing lasting relationships and ran away from anyone who tried to get close. I began hanging around the wrong crowd and starting drinking. I craved the feeling of disconnectedness alcohol gave me. I found a sense of family with the new friends I had made. I needed an increasing amount of alcohol to feel better. Even though it was a temporary escape, I took it. Somehow, I managed to keep up with school and even hold down a job. It wasn't long before I was introduced to cocaine, and that led to more drinking. I eventually grew tired of hangovers and realized that no matter how much I drank and tried to destroy myself, things were always the same in the morning.

As high school unfolded, I focused more on school and began purging destructive relationships. I convinced myself that the only way to survive was to take on the world by myself. Over the years, I had become very intolerant of people. I walked away from people and experiences and never looked back. If I didn't become attached, then no one could hurt me. Even things that weren't final seemed final to me. I wanted it all to seem final.

Like everyone else, I wanted to find happiness, but I had no idea how to do it. Despite being surrounded by family, friends, and the occasional boyfriend, I knew in my heart that something was missing. It wasn't until I was thirty-three that I finally signed up for Confirmation classes, hoping that I would find a better way of coping. Confirmation yields graces, but the effects of those graces aren't immediately seen.

I finished college and entered the field of pediatric nursing. I had finally found something that I excelled at. I enjoyed making sick children laugh and loved seeing the smiles on their faces. Soon after, I met my husband at work, and I immediately knew he was different. Unlike previous relationships, this one gave me a sense of safety. I let my guard down for the first time. One day, he mentioned that his dad had signed them up for a retreat and that they would be leaving for a few days. They would not have outside contact during the retreat.

My boyfriend embraced the retreat experience. The weekend passed, and it was time to meet the men after Sunday Mass.

The weekend away from him helped me realize that this guy could be the one. As the men started walking in, I barely recognized some of them. They looked so different. The worry on their faces had been replaced by peace and tranquility. I was in awe of how different they looked in a matter of three days.

Now, I wanted to experience what they had experienced. I asked my boyfriend for details, but he just said that I should make my own retreat. I wasn't sure what ACTS Retreats were all about, but I was going to find out. After making some calls, they told me that they were held for men, women, and teens, so I tried signing up for the women's retreat. To my frustration, every time I tried to sign up, all the slots were already filled.

I got busy with life and distracted by my newfound happiness. We married and had our first daughter. I felt incredibly blessed, but somewhere in the back of my mind, I still had that darkness weighing me down. I was fine one minute, then overcome with sadness another. I began to feel dread — dread I would be a bad mother and a bad wife. I began to fear that others would see my unworthiness, and I would lose everything I held dear. I began to have nightmares again, vivid nightmares of blood and water.

While I had told my husband a few minor details of my past, I was not ready to share with him the heaviness I continued to feel. I turned to a friend at work who knew us both very well and had been a catalyst for our relationship. I gave her a few details. She encouraged me to heal my inner child. She felt that the birth of my baby had forced me to address unresolved hurts in my own childhood. She asked if I had ever been to an ACTS Retreat (Adoration, Community, Theology, and Service) and went on to say that she and her husband had seen many people heal from past hurts through this retreat. I told her I had tried to sign up for a retreat, but the timing never seemed to work. As it turned out, she was on the team for the next women's retreat with her church, but they were already full. Then one day my friend told me that one of the retreatants was unable to go, and there was an open slot — but she needed an answer quickly.

My daughter was only six months old, and I wondered whether leaving her was a good idea. My husband assured me that the baby would be fine and insisted I go. As I left for the retreat, I prayed it would make me whole again. I wanted to feel better so that I could be better for my husband and daughter. I also wanted to be better for me. The God who made me wanted to teach me, lead me, and heal me.

The weekend surpassed my expectations. I witnessed regular women with a capacity to love the stranger in a way I never knew was possible. Over the years I heard that God loves us and his mercy is boundless, that he patiently waits for us to seek him. That weekend I experienced God's love and mercy. God slowly filled my soul with his peace.

The drive home after the retreat was so different. The noise from the traffic and the hustle and bustle around me seemed frenetic and loud. I immediately began to miss the peace and tranquility of the past few days. But they gave us tools over the weekend that prepared us to take on the world differently. It would be up to me to continue to build on my relationship with Christ.

My husband was happy to see that the retreat had brought me so much joy. We baptized our daughter, and life continued. I planned to attend the follow-up meetings after the retreat, but I let work get in the way. A sense of despair returned. We had two beautiful little girls now, and I had so many things to be grateful for, but fear had returned. A sense of hopelessness and loneliness slowly cast a dark shadow over all the good things God had given me.

I spent incredible energy trying to appear happy and to convince everyone that we had a normal life, but I was dying inside. I felt like a failure as a mother and took on more work, thinking that my daughters didn't really need me around. I wanted to contribute more financially, which made no sense because my children were little and had no real concept of material things anyway. I still was afraid that if my husband really knew me, he'd see that I was damaged and that nothing good could come of me. If the kids didn't want to be with me, I took it personally. I took everything personally.

I checked out. I began drinking again and was constantly thinking that I would be better off dead than feeling worthless. One day in frustration that my youngest didn't want to go to the store with me, I told my husband that the family would be better off without me. They would have the opportunity to have a better mom and a better wife. His puzzled look and his words of reassurance confused me. I began to distance myself. I kept up with all my responsibilities and relationships, but the emptiness was numbing. I tried to fall back on coping mechanisms that I had acquired in sessions with my clinical psychologist years before I was married, but nothing helped.

My husband had been ill with leukemia when he was thirty, almost ten years before I met him. He began having severe back pain, and the doctors were sure his cancer was back, but they couldn't figure out where. I felt guilty for having allowed myself to wander away from God. I begged for his forgiveness and asked for strength. I asked him to help me accept this cross if it was his will and to give me the courage to trust him. My husband is a wonderful man — not just a great husband, but a wonderful father, son, brother, uncle, and friend to so many. For the first time, I realized that at some point in my life, God had deemed me worthy of this man.

I asked others to pray, and I also began praying that something other than cancer was causing his pain. After several exams to rule out a cancer relapse, he was diagnosed with a torn disc. He had surgery and came home.

We settled back into life, but God wanted me to keep healing. He had my attention, and he didn't want me to return to old patterns of coping. One day, my phone rang, and it was my friend's sister. She said she was sorry to bother me so soon after my husband's surgery, but she needed to ask me something. She wondered whether I would be interested in being part of the team leading an upcoming retreat.

I told her I would be thrilled to join the team. The meetings began, and I soon realized what went on behind the scenes to make a retreat possible. There was a lot of spiritual preparation, planning, and work. While it was not a perfect process, it was certainly opening my eyes to a different way of life, a way of loving service. The women who had worked retreats in the past reassured me that I just needed to trust that God would guide and direct us. I was amazed at their confidence. Trust … that was certainly a new way of living. I realized that I had more to learn here than my role on this retreat.

As I struggled with my fears and reservations, I recognized my need for some direction. I was very comfortable with one member of the team. She had a grace about her, the kind of charism that indicated she was the right person to turn to, and she spoke so beautifully about our Lord and about our Blessed Mother. I could trust her. Trusting her was a way of trusting myself with God.

I began the painful process of sharing my story and giving life to emotions that had been stuffed down for so long. As the words tumbled out, I felt the pain all over again — the pain of what had happened and the pain of the things that had come as a result. Once I started, I couldn't stop. But as the words left my mouth, I could feel something changing inside me. I could feel myself making room for better things.

Making room.

It was a key to getting out of the stuck place. I needed to make room for God's goodness. When I finished telling my story, my friend faced me squarely. She was crying. I had a hard time accepting that those tears were shed for my pain, and yet there I stood, in the most vulnerable moment of my life. She was helping me to carry the weight of an old cross.

She hugged me and said the words that would stay with me: "I'm so sorry. I'm so sorry all those terrible things happened to you and no one helped you. I'm sorry." Even as I type these

> *"The only appropriate response to*
> *another human person is love."*
> *Saint John Paul II*
>
> Patty's experience in sharing her story with her mother shows us the dangers survivors can face when telling their story. The reaction of the listener has the potential to exacerbate the trauma. It can cause a greater sense of hopelessness, abandonment, rejection, and self-hatred. A non-loving and non-accepting reaction can introduce even more complexity into the trauma.
>
> Patty's sharing with the person from church also shows how the listener's reaction can be healing, imparting Christ's unconditional love. When we listen to stories of trauma, our reaction should be a witness to how Christ sees the survivor. It can show that they are worthy of love. This example teaches us how to listen and provide empathy.
>
> Most importantly, the listener must be present. The listener is there as a person who can validate the experiences and emotions. The listener can also share emotions. They can cry with the survivor. They can walk together through a story. They can even hug them (but only after asking permission first!).

words, my eyes fill up with tears as I remember that moment. Years of therapy, counseling, self-help books ... yet nothing had healed me like this moment. I just cried as something dark and heavy left my body. For the first time in my life, someone had acknowledged that I had been hurt, that those things should not have happened to me, and that it was not my fault. She became Simon of Cyrene, stepping under the weight of my cross, and carrying it for me.

She became Veronica, wiping my tears.

She became Mary Magdalene, spilling precious perfumed oil into my soul.

In that moment, I knew that I was good. I still am God's beautiful creation. And he makes all things new. One genuine act of kindness had managed to take a space that had been filled with shame, doubt, and fear and instantly fill it with love. I will be eternally grateful to her for everything that happened in that mysterious and miraculous moment.

It was a change that stayed, and a peace that didn't fade. It was a kind of liberty for the captives. A release from darkness for those who have been held hostage. A day in which the oppressed are set free. My friend had been Christ to me in order to lead me to the abundant life of Christ — the life he wants us all to live.

Where sin increased, grace abounded more.

PRAYER

Heavenly Father,

Thank you for the many times that you have saved me. Thank you for sending angels to descend upon me during the darkest, weakest moments in my life. My past hurts have scarred me, but I have learned to embrace them because they helped me to understand more fully your mercy and grace.

The crosses I encountered brought me back to you, Lord.

I pray that every child might come to know your love and

your mother's love while they are still young so that they might know that no matter what happens to them here on earth, no matter who hurts them or who fails them, they have your mother and a heavenly Father who will always love them, strengthen them, and guide them along the path to your great love, which reaches out to all souls, heals all wounds, redeems all things.

Amen.

WALKING TOGETHER WITH EMPATHY

Think of empathy as "walking with."

Theresa Wiseman, a licensed nurse who has contributed to psychological research, defines empathy with four attributes:

- to be able to see the world as others see it
- to be nonjudgmental
- to understand another person's feelings
- to communicate your understanding of that person's feelings

Truly being empathic is not easy. It requires us to be able to see the world as others see it. It requires us to lay aside our judgmental nature. It requires us to walk in a different pair of shoes. And in the case of survivors of sexual trauma, empathy requires us to communicate our understanding of their feelings back to the survivor (Wiseman, 1996).

Most survivors have developed a deep sense of shame. Brené Brown gave a TED Talk in which she points out that shame loses its power when we respond with true empathy to someone sharing their experience.

Empathy is the antidote to shame.

Empathy is the antidote, not sympathy. This distinction is incredibly important. Empathy is willing to hear the survivor's story, to have a true desire to understand their experiences, and walk with them through their pain. Sympathy is simply a detached expression of sorrow or pity for someone else, without being willing to walk with them in their suffering. The listener must stay away from blame, judgment, shame, guilt, and sympathy. Sympathy is powerless to help the survivor. It seems devoid of any meaning or care.

Too many survivors have left the Church because of listeners not having empathy. The survivor was instead faced with judgment or criticism, or with emotional distance and a lack of someone there to walk with them. Their shame and guilt were exacerbated to the point of fleeing.

Sometimes, we are called to be Simon of Cyrene.

MARGUERITE'S STORY

I was raped on March 15, 2006, a day seared in my memory.

I was in graduate school in Washington, DC, at the time. My best friend and I had decided that we would go on a cruise together to Mexico during my spring break. The ship left from California, but Erin lived in Arizona. The plan was for me to fly from DC to Arizona, and then Erin and I would drive from Arizona to California. The day before I was supposed to fly into Arizona, Erin was pulled over for speeding. The police officer scanned Erin's license, informed her that her license had been suspended due to an unpaid ticket, and towed away Erin's car. Suddenly, our simple plan of driving from Arizona to California became an almost insurmountable obstacle. We tried everything we could think of to get to the port of departure. We finally found a rental car company that did not scan Erin's license to see if it was active, so they rented a car to Erin. I was elated. We were smarter than the system.

So many times I look back and wonder why I pushed so hard. I was like a bull with my horns down, determined to go forward despite any obstacles in my path. In the Book of Psalms, the psalmist uses the word *Selah* seventy-one times. Selah is a Hebrew word that means something equivalent to "stop and listen." What a beautiful image of what I should have done. I do not blame myself for the rape — it was not my fault. I know that with every fiber of my being. However, to tell my story truthfully, I must share how God was trying to talk to me through those initial frustrations to our travel plans. I did not stop to listen, yet God was there. He was in that moment, but I missed him.

Erin and I made it onto the cruise ship. On the night of March 15, we decided to get dressed up and enjoy the nightlife onboard. I put on a backless black dress and black high heels, and I felt beautiful. Erin and I went to one of the lounge areas aboard the cruise ship, had some drinks, and started talking to some men our age. Toward the end of the night, Erin was tired and wanted to go back to our cabin. I decided to stay up a while longer and continue to enjoy the conversations and male attention. After Erin went back to our cabin, one of the men put Rohypnol in my drink without my knowledge. Rohypnol is more commonly known as the "date rape" drug. It is about ten times stronger than Valium and takes effect very quickly. After I unknowingly consumed the Rohypnol, I passed out.

I woke up the next morning cold and wet, lying on my back in a strange cabin. As I became more conscious, I realized that I was naked, lying in a pool of blood and urine with black and blue marks on my arms from being held down. There were three men in the room. I recognized one of the men from the night before. In shock, confused and filled with overwhelming terror, I grabbed my clothes and left as quickly as I could to return to my cabin and find Erin.

I told my friend what had happened, but I did not report the rape to the authorities on the cruise ship because I was in a state of shock. My mind could not process what had occurred. I figured out that the man had violated me. I was bleeding, but I couldn't understand why I had no memory. I would never have agreed to have sex with this man. At this point, I wasn't even able to wrap my mind around the word rape or explain the memory lapse due to the Rohypnol. I think this is why so many rape survivors make excuses for perpetrators and blame themselves for the event. Our brains are not equipped to process traumatic events immediately. It is easier to pretend the rape didn't occur, that maybe it was something else, and we search for logical explanations for the violation.

I actually considered going back to the man and having sex with him consensually. This behavior sounds insane to someone who has never experienced rape, but I wanted to put the pieces together in a way that made sense to me, I felt compelled to recreate the exact same event so that I could insert my choice, my free will, into the scene. In my mixed-up mind, I thought doing this would allow me to erase the event that had occurred without my choice. I had lost all control over my body and was struggling to get some power back, and I had no idea how to do that. I thought I could somehow take control of the situation by having sex with the man consensually.

Erin convinced me not to follow through on this irrational way of regaining control. She also tried to persuade me not to talk to him. I did it anyway. I went up to the man and asked him if we'd had sex. He responded with a cool yes. What I already knew and feared the most had been confirmed. Slowly, I realized what had happened. At this point, I was at the beginning of an incredibly long and arduous journey. I had a million miles ahead of me to healing, but I had taken the first step: I had admitted to myself that I had been raped. I had been violated. I had been completely unable to give consent. The man had stolen my ability to say no.

When I arrived back in Washington, I told a few family members and friends what had occurred. Two men became pivotal in my life: my friend Chris, and my brother, Kevin. Chris had experienced a lot of significant suffering in his life. Suffering can either harden our hearts and make us bitter, or it can soften our hearts and make us empathetic. Chris was empathetic. After I confided in him about the rape, Chris began sending me daily text messages, telling me that he was thinking about me and was available to talk. Chris sent me these daily text messages for six months. The messages were kind, gentle. Chris invited me to contact him if I needed to talk to someone. Through his daily offering of self, I began to realize that Chris genuinely cared, and he was ready to help bear my suffering. I would call Chris most often in the middle of the night. Nights were very difficult for me. I could not sleep because I was paralyzed with fear, and now I was suffering from Post Traumatic Stress Disorder (PTSD). When I called, Chris would always wake up and talk to me. Sometimes he would pretend that he was already awake, even though it was the middle of the night. Chris became my rock.

Kevin flooded me with kindness and encouragement. He frequently mailed me cards. The messages were often very simple, usually saying, "I love you," "I miss you," or "I'm thinking about you." Kevin also began to send me closed stargazer lilies on a regular basis. I would put the lilies in water and watch them slowly bloom. Every day when I got home from graduate school, I would walk into the kitchen, look at my flowers, and find them a little bit more open than the previous day. Watching the flowers bloom gave me hope. Watching this process happen over and over again helped me to realize that it was possible for my life to open and flower again.

CHECKING IN

Once a survivor has given you the privilege of their trust and vulnerability by sharing their story with you, you must respect that gift. If you are able to (and you might not be because of boundaries), reach out to them on a consistent basis. This could be once a week or once a month. It could be as simple as "Hi, I'm thinking about you and wanted to check in?" or "Hi, just thinking about you and reminding you that I am here if you need anything."

It's helpful to check in even a year later and many years after that. Trauma like this is not easily forgotten and comes up more than the survivor would like. Checking in, even long after stories were shared, can be really reassuring. It can be a reminder that it's okay to still be struggling with the trauma. It can be validating that someone knows that it's a daily struggle.

Everything about my life changed after the rape. I was in a living hell, and suffering from PTSD. The foods that I liked changed, I stopped feeling sexually attracted to men and started feeling sexually attracted to women, and I was terrified all of the time. I could not sleep, and I gained weight. I did not recognize myself. That was terrifying. After all, there is one person in life who is constant, always there: you. You are always you.

But I was not me. I didn't recognize myself.

In general, you know who you are. You know what kind of foods you like, you know who you are attracted to, and you know your personality. For me, that had changed. I had gone through a horrifying experience where I had lost all control, and after that, I lost the familiarity of knowing who I was. I morphed.

Adapted. I changed. And everything got confused.

The biggest change was the fear. Crushing fear. I had experienced a random act of violence, and any sense of security or safety that I had felt before the event disappeared. I did not have a guarantee that another act of personal physical violence would not happen to me tomorrow. I was afraid that someone was going to attack me if I walked down a street. I was scared that someone was going to break into my house. I could not sleep.

I was most afraid of men. It was physically impossible for me to feel sexually attracted to men. We were like oil and water. I no longer sensed joy in the complementarity of man and woman. However, I was still a sexual being. I began to feel sexually attracted to women. I found myself looking at women and feeling the spark of desire that I had previously felt toward men. I was confused and overwhelmed. I felt abandoned by God.

It is a heart-wrenching experience to feel that God has abandoned you. Like Jesus on the cross, my heart cried out, "My God, my God, why have you forsaken me?" (Mt 27:46). I had deeply loved God and trusted in him my whole life. Now that I had been raped, though, I was paralyzed by fear, and I was experiencing sexual attraction toward women. It seemed like I was never going to be able to overcome all the obstacles in my journey to wholeness. The life I once knew, a life of safety and consolation in following Jesus, was gone.

Those who have been violated sometimes lose their appetite. Sometimes they gain weight. I gained weight, for a variety of reasons. The main reason I gained weight was because I hated my body. I wondered whether my body was what had motivated the rapist to attack me. I now know that rape is a crime motivated by power, control, anger, domination, and violence. It has nothing to do with sexual desire. But at the time, I yearned to feel safe again. The period after the rape was very difficult for me, because I wanted to ensure that I would never be raped again, but I had not done anything to cause the rape to happen in the first place. So how could I prevent it from happening twice? I tried to take away any sexual attraction men might feel for me, hoping that gaining weight would prevent sexual assault.

I knew that I needed psychological help, so I started seeing a therapist at DC Rape Crisis Center. The therapist was vital in my psychological healing. But every time I thought about God, I felt betrayed and lost. It was impossible for me to believe that a loving God could allow such personal physical violence to happen. I was living in a spiritual paradox: I felt betrayed by God, but I knew that I needed him.

While I was in graduate school, a priest would come and celebrate Mass in the school's chapel. I happened to have a one-hour break in my schedule every day at noon, so I started going to daily Mass. I would just sit in Mass and stare. My body was at Mass, but my heart felt totally numb.

One day at Mass during the consecration, when the priest held the host and said, "This is my body," I had a vision of Jesus. He was naked, lying in a pool of blood and urine, with black and blue marks on his arms. The image filled me with disgust. The same vision came to me the next day at Mass. Again, the third day, I had the same vision at the same moment in the Mass. The vision recurred for many days.

In time, I realized that Jesus was in the same position I had been in when I woke up from the rape, naked, lying in a pool of blood and urine, with black and blue marks on my arms from having been held down. I finally realized what Jesus was telling me: He suffered with me.

When the priest held up the host and said, "This is my body," Jesus was saying in a very intimate way that not only is the Eucharist his body, but I am part of his body. In Holy Communion, we become one both physically and spiritually. When I suffer, he suffers. When I was raped, he was raped.

In the Book of Acts, Saul (who became Paul) persecuted Christians. Then Jesus appeared to Saul in a vision and said, "Saul, Saul, why are you persecuting me?" When we are hurt, Jesus is hurt.

I even began to understand why God had permitted the rape. Jesus has given each person free will, so when the rapist made the free choice to rape me, Jesus did not take away his free will; instead, Jesus suffered with me. Some people exercise their free will by choosing to do evil. When one of Christ's members is hurt — persecuted, raped, killed — Jesus' own heart is pierced.

Jesus loves me so much that he was not watching from a distance while I was raped. He was right there.

The vision of Jesus at Mass was a turning point for me, and the beginning of my spiritual healing process. I started to see that God loves me so much that he entered into my pain, he was present in my trauma, and that this loving God would not revoke the free will he had given to every person. But even then, his Sacred Heart would triumph. I still felt broken, lost, and scared, but I knew that I needed God to heal me spiritually.

I started to read the Bible. I felt God leading me toward passages about Jerusalem. Throughout history, Jerusalem has been conquered, raped, pillaged, and plundered. It has been destroyed and rebuilt again. Yet it is still precious to the Lord. It is a holy place. Jerusalem plays an important part in God's deliverance. God began to show me how those who have been raped are like Jerusalem. But that is not the end of God's plan. We are precious to the Lord, and he wants us to play an important part in deliverance. I began to substitute my name for the words "Jerusalem," "Israel," or "Zion" when I read Sacred Scripture. I read the passages slowly and listened to what God was saying. These passages have become so dear to me: Isaiah 62:1–5, Zephaniah 3:14–20, and Revelation 21:1–5a.

I am his beloved. And he is mine. He fights for me. He rejoices in me. He protects and shelters me. He comforts me. He will restore me.

CREATING COMMUNITY

"Our brains are built to help us function as members of a tribe" ("The body keeps the score: Brain, mind, and body in the healing of trauma," Bessel A. van der Kolk, American Psychological Association, 2014).

For many survivors, the natural sense of tribe has been taken away. To them, there is no sense of community, let alone the sense of a safe community. To live in trauma is to be alone. Gatherings cause sensations of too many unknowns, too many people, and too much danger.

You can provide reassurance by walking with the survivor. Gently and calmly assist them with rejoining community activities. Encourage them while providing space. Let them know that they are in control of the timing and level of involvement. Help them find safe and enjoyable church and community activities to partake in.

Invite them along to activities with you. Going by themselves may be too overwhelming. You can be an anchor. Remember, the survivor may not know how to trust. A simple encounter with others can lead to a lot of questions about self and feelings of not being good enough, being criticized, and being unwelcome. It's important that you are there to help answer these questions and provide support. Be their anchor.

I transferred from the graduate school I was attending in Washington, DC, to another graduate school in Austin, Texas, in order to be closer to my family and friends for support. I received a call from the director of Cedarbrake Retreat Center, Brian Egan. Brian informed me that Cedarbrake was going to put on a retreat called Healing Hearts for women who had been raped, and he invited me to come.

Even though Sacred Scripture was helping me to see God as a loving God, I still struggled. I was not the person I had been before the rape, and I did not know what it would take to feel whole again. I knew it would have to be extraordinary. I needed a transformation of heart and a complete healing in my relationship with God. The visions at Mass had started the healing. Sacred Scripture had helped me to understand that God loves me. But I still was not healed. I was not whole.

I attended Healing Hearts retreat with twenty-five other women of all ages and many different nationalities. Some of the women were pregnant. Even though we looked very different on the outside, all of us bore the same deep scars. Those women were more similar to me than people I had previously encountered in my life. We were different people, but we were also the exact same person. Trauma and violation had changed us.

The retreat was beautiful. We shared stories and found community with each other. We were prayed over individually, and received the Sacrament of the Anointing of the Sick. We were given blessed teddy bears to sleep with, because nighttime is when PTSD symptoms manifest most often. Above all, we experienced God's healing and love in a very profound way. At the end of the retreat, although we still bore the permanent scars that reminded us of what we had suffered, they were no longer bleeding wounds. God had transformed our open wounds into healed scars. I left the retreat no longer feeling broken, but feeling whole again. My relationship with God had been mended. I was finally at peace.

Other resources assisted in my healing process. Books, songs (secular and sacred), and sacred art were all instrumental in my journey.

My sexual attraction to men gradually returned, and in 2011 I married my husband, Tommy. After I was raped, if someone had told me that I would eventually get married, I would not have believed him. I was convinced it was impossible that I could ever love, trust, and feel safe with a man again. Marriage is not the right choice for every rape survivor, but if the desire to be married is buried deep in your heart, just know that it is possible. The rape was one time, but Tommy's strength and love renews me every day.

Two years after I married Tommy, I was praying at Eucharistic adoration when I felt God calling me to tell the story of my rape and my healing. Following God's promptings, I contacted Raymond Arroyo at EWTN, the global Catholic television network. Raymond listened to my story and invited me to be a guest on EWTN's weekly live news program, *The World Over Live*, which is broadcast to more than two hundred million homes on six continents. On April 4, 2013, I was interviewed on the show and told a condensed version of my rape and healing.

TAKING ACTION

Sexual abuse is a problem. We can all take actions to help. As someone in the Church community, you can take action. Whether you are a layperson, clergy, or working in ministry, make an effort to create change. You can help bring awareness to the fact that sexual abuse happens and that it could be occurring in the community. You can help publicize the signs, and encourage everyone to be vigilant and aware. You can encourage victims to reach out for support.

You can offer resources, start a support group, or offer Mass for those who have been sexually abused. Let the community know that abuse will not be tolerated. Let them know that you are there to provide support. Giving the survivor the ability to see real action taking place can help bring back a sense of safety and agency: Something is being done, and they are not alone.

Sexual trauma can cause survivors to imagine that their relationship with God has been broken. Seeing the Church come together can help rebuild that image of Christ and his loving kindness. Seeing the Church unite and take action can help show that God is there for them.

Healing from being raped is a process that spans a lifetime. I am in a much better place than I once was, though I am not the person I was before the rape. I do know that I am precious to Jesus, and I know he has a very special plan for my life. He gives us what we need, if we ask. He even gives us what we need when we don't know how to ask.

PRAYER

Dear Jesus, the Great Healer,

I am scared. I try to be strong and I desire to bring hope to others, but deep in my heart I still find it difficult to trust you. There are so many walls surrounding my heart. I struggle to let you in completely. Thank you for loving me, for suffering with me, and for restoring me.

I praise you for all of your profound experiences of healing and love in my life. Please help me to believe that your love surrounds me, and to feel safe once again that I might fall into your arms. I don't want to be scared anymore. I want to trust in you, to believe, and to be free to give myself to you completely.

I need your help. Be my strength when I am weak, be my feet when I can't walk, and be my heart when I can't love. I want to love you wholly, without any reservation or any fear, for the rest of my life.

Amen.

REPORT!

One of the first things a listener often wants to suggest is that the survivor report the abuse. Be careful!

Do not pressure the survivor to report. You can suggest it, but don't pressure them into it. Never ask "why didn't you report them already?" This seems like the logical thing to do from the outside, but there are many reasons the survivor has chosen not to report yet.

Like Marguerite said, she didn't report because she couldn't really remember what happened or how to make sense of it. Like I mentioned previously, trauma often gets remembered in fragments. The brain often dissociates from the experience. If drugs were involved, there may be a huge black hole in the memory. The human brain is not designed to endure that kind of trauma. Trauma causes the brain great confusion, intrusion, and a myriad of emotions and physical sensations. It can be almost impossible to even begin to formulate a coherent story, let alone report it.

There are many unknowns with reporting. *Will they believe me? What if they tell me it was my fault? What if they don't do anything about it?*

If you do suggest making a report, offer to be there with them. Being in a police station or having to answer a bunch of invasive questions to which they may or may not have the answers can add even more complexity to the trauma. The reassuring presence of a trusted person can be extremely helpful.

While it is important not to pressure the survivor into reporting, you need to allow the survivor to realize they have the power to make a choice. This knowledge of empowerment is vital. They have the power to decide if they want to do something. Doing something could be reporting, but that may feel too scary. Present them options and as many choices as possible, where they can actively choose and assert both their "yes" and "no."

Please note that any abuse reported to a diocese will be sent to authorities, as dioceses are mandated reporters.

The most helpful thing you can do is offer your support and your presence.

JEANETTE'S STORY

I am the first of four children born within five years. My parents had farming backgrounds and loved to dance, and that is how they met. In my cache of pictures, I find only two of my dad: one of their wedding day and one with me as a toddler. I have no memory of my father being with us or holding any of my siblings. Though he lived in the same Iowa town, he was a ghost to us, except an occasional phone call and promise to visit that never materialized. There was another family who also had four children living in our town. Our mothers spent a lot of time together and were often out searching for the men who did not come home, did not work, but continually found other women to charm. In the end, my dad married five times.

When I started kindergarten, Mom and the four of us lived in a two-room house. Dad came by one night and slept in bed with Mom and me. He did things to her I didn't fully understand. I was frozen and motionless, a child in a world she did not understand. When I saw him two years later, he was in a fit of rage. He yelled at Mom, demanded money, and refused to believe her when she said she didn't have any. He pushed her to the floor, broke her glasses, and grabbed the kitchen butcher knife and held it to her throat. She was crying and yelling at him. My siblings and I were terrified. Finally, I ran to the phone to call the police, but I could not find the number ("911" wouldn't exist for another twenty years). By the time I got back to the kitchen, he was gone.

Trauma. Sexuality. Violence. I had been exposed to them all, and I was only five.

On the Fourth of July one year, my three-year-old brother and I were sitting in the basement in a circle with some other kids, and my dad's twenty-year-old brother was there, touching himself in front of us. We left the basement, and I was ready to tell Mom what had happened, but by now my young uncle was playing with fireworks and there was an explosion. A firecracker split the side of his nose open. I tried to get Mom's attention, but everyone was making a fuss over his face and the blood, and so the little girl went unnoticed. That impression began a repulsion for the male anatomy that would last a long time.

Again, violence, trauma, and sexuality converged. And I was still so young.

Mom was a hard worker and used all her strength and skills to can food, bake bread, sew clothes, and work full-time as a line operator in a factory. Relatives rejected our little family because of my parents' divorce. No one from either side of the family showed up to visit, nor were we invited to anyone's house. We did not know our neighbors because renting to a divorcee was taboo, and we moved seven times before I started high school. Every week Mom would drive to the courthouse to pick up her child-support check. She sent me in to get it while she stayed in the car with the other kids. It was supposed to be twenty dollars, but most of the time it was not there. She never said a word, but I absorbed her angst. Somehow, she remained faithful to Sunday Mass and negotiated tuition for us to attend Catholic schools in the elementary grades.

There was something about a man, twenty dollars, and a break in trust that would stick with me. It wasn't the last time in my life that these things would go together.

My mom met a military fella at the Saturday night dances. They dated for some time, and when he came by the house, he was always engaging and fun. At Christmastime he sent us gifts from Okinawa, where he was stationed. It was an unbelievable thrill to get presents, and we were hoping he would be our new dad! But that was the last we heard from him. He was just gone.

Then I turned nine, and Mom befriended the wife and mother of a family of eight. In the beginning it was so much fun to have kids to play with, and we spent a lot of time at their house. After a few months the older kids tried to pull me into a game of strip poker, but I refused to join them, and they labeled me as that "Catholic girl." Then one day I walked up to the enclosed front porch, and their dad opened the door with himself fully exposed. I ran away as fast as I could. My siblings and I were often alone because mom worked, and I babysat. I became reticent about going to the house with all of the children and absolutely refused to go if their father was going to be there; and then the visits just stopped. Little did I know that he had sexually abused my two younger sisters, Rosie and Kathy, who at the time were four and six. Forty years later, I learned that a local doctor and my mother had him committed to an insane asylum, where he stayed until he died.

Sexual violation and predatory experiences. They had not only damaged me; they had now spread to my siblings. Predators look at vulnerable families like ours, families filled with hungry hope for friendship and true companions on the journey of life, and they see vulnerability.

My sweet little sisters became caught up in distressed lives with abusive men, and they died at fifty and fifty-seven. I had moved away when I was seventeen, so I did not witness the degree of their suffering, but I saw the effects of it in everyday anxiety, depression, self-abuses like scratching the skin on their arms till they bled, other addictions, and finally diabetes and pancreatic cancer. They tried to care for others, but they did not know how to care for themselves, and the men they attracted were all takers.

Our only brother, Jim, was bounced from pillar to post trying to navigate his anger. He told me when he was five that he was going to get Dad for what he had seen the day I tried to call the police and couldn't find the number. My brother acted out through his teen years and was sent to Boystown, but he encountered many abuses in his cottage, so he turned to weight-lifting to survive. He ran away from there and kept running until he was fifty, when he decided to stop fighting it. He turned to drinking. The last two years of his life were spent in a nursing home from two strokes and several debilitating diseases. He carried a lifetime of pain, but we began to share honestly two years before I lost him. He returned to the Church four months before he died.

When I was eleven, my mom married for the second time. Before this, it had been normal for me to hop into her bed on Saturday mornings. On one particular day after her remarriage, I did not know she had gone into work. Mom's new husband invited me into the bed. At first, I felt happy to know he seemed to care about us kids, but that suddenly changed as he explored my developing body with his hands. I froze in fear. He said, "If you ever tell your mom, I will kill you!" Since she did not have to go into work on a Saturday again, I was never alone with him, but the experience left me in a constant state of anxiety. Within six months of the marriage, he just disappeared. I remembered his vicious threat, and it took fifteen years for me to tell Mom. She sighed and said he was no good.

Violation. False intimacy. Lies. And a response that lacked substantive help. It was time for some grace. God knew I needed it.

We were in St. Mary's School at that time, and it was a safe place to go, with Franciscan nuns who were kind. We had Eucharistic processions through the neighborhoods at night with candles, and people sang hymns and prayed the Rosary. I became a Lady of the Altar in seventh grade and would linger after the other girls left just so I could do extra tasks in the sanctuary where I felt peace and close to God in the quiet. I made my First Holy Communion at this parish, and I remember it being the happiest I had ever been. As I approached the altar rail, everyone else just faded away; it was only Jesus and me and a wave of love. That cherished memory would come back to me down the road when I was far, far away from God.

Through St. Mary's School, I met a wonderful teacher, Frances. She had been a lead ballerina in the Chicago ballet for Swan Lake. Her four children went to St. Mary's, and she taught ballet to all who were interested. I was immediately taken in by the beauty of expressive dance. Having grown up on country music and polkas, I was now hearing classical music, and I wanted to be near it, near her, and dancing my life away. Already five feet seven (heading for five feet nine) with a large frame, I found that was not to be my calling, but I became friends with her family and was their regular babysitter at thirteen.

It was always fun being at their house, and the kids loved me. Her strong and friendly policeman husband included me in all conversations, and I felt respected. When we moved across town, he always picked me up and drove me home. He seemed eager to help Mom by chauffeuring me around. He began giving me small gifts. Then he gave me twenty dollars to buy a dress for a performance I was in, and another twenty dollars for round-trip bus fare to go to St. Louis over Thanksgiving to visit friends from my childhood. Just before the trip, he drove me a different way home. It was dark and snowing, and he turned down a gravel road. He stopped the car. My heart was beating fast. Then he turned me toward himself and kissed me. I had not been kissed before. Actually, no one in my life gave affection in those days, not even my mother, so in the moment it felt good, but I also felt conflicted and did not know what to say or do. He started up the car and drove the rest of the way in silence. I left the next day for Thanksgiving in Missouri but did not return as prearranged. I was having fun with my adopted cousins and did not want to leave. Mom called. She was angry. The next day, I got on the bus.

Once I got home, Mom and I did not talk. I took thirty aspirin and went to bed, hoping to never wake up. The next day I did wake up, groggy, but still alive. I heard voices downstairs, and when I came down, I saw a police officer across from my mom. I knew something was going on, because Mom should have been at work. They stopped talking when I walked into the room. Then he began to question me: Had Officer Brown touched me? No, I lied. I had been threatened with death if I spoke about what happened when I was eleven, and I felt myself in the same emotional trap. The police officer asked me several more times, in different ways, but I stayed with my story. I was confused and scared, yet somehow devoted to that family. A little while later, they moved across the country, and I never heard from them again. Mom didn't bring it up after that.

The same grip held me. It seemed to define me. Stay quiet. The trauma will come and go. Let the confusion and betrayal sit with you. There is no way out of this. It just is. Twenty dollars for your soul. Twenty dollars for your peace of mind. Twenty dollars — something akin to thirty pieces of silver.

The following summer, Mom married again, just before I began high school. We moved into his three-bedroom rambler with one of his three older children still there and a baby sister on the way. Survival looked much different from what we had previously learned, and we now were taught a new form of abuse. Physical. Emotional. A cycle of fighting, running away, crying, and confusion. It was a constant state of anxiety. Dating became my outlet and an uncharted sea of feelings and longing.

I was looking for something. God was looking for me.

At seventeen, I attended a three-day retreat at school. Each day the priest invited us to confession. It was not on my radar to go, but then Mom and I had a fight, and she slapped me in the face. I went to confess what a bad person I was, and the priest said, "You are a good girl!" I had never heard those words in my life. He kept in contact, and the following summer he arranged for me to move to Omaha and live as a mother's helper to a family with six children under the age of eight. They arranged for my tuition to be paid my senior year, a convincing reason for me to stay and no longer be a burden to my stepdad.

I went from getting D's as a junior to getting on the honor roll. The new environment was affirming and provided a much healthier picture of life; but I carried with me the instability of trauma and struggled with confidence. That family moved to Pennsylvania, and I was on my own. I found a job that opened a door to move to the East Coast, and I was ready to go. But that was different from being *prepared* to go. I was so accustomed to living in the mode of "fight, flight, or freeze" that I fell for anyone who hinted at love or who might take care of me. When I was twenty-one years old, I met a handsome man in the advertising world. He had an engaging personality, and he took me to fine places for dinner, theaters on Broadway, and regular trips to the Caribbean. He also gave me beautiful jewelry. I was never alone and thought I was safe in this relationship, even though he was forty-eight.

Within a few years, I was on an exam table in a New York City Planned Parenthood for the first of two abortions, just nine months apart. I remember being anxious and feeling lost, for unmarried pregnant girls were publicly shunned where I came from. The words that were tearing at my heart were: "I do not want to raise a child the way I was." I never said those words out loud, but the suppressed anger of more than twenty years erupted in that terrible moment of fear, and I did not turn away. Then the room blurred, and I was plunged into a well of pain I had never known and a wound to my soul that would not be healed for thirty-three years.

I attempted suicide, drank too much, and could not reconcile the relationship I was living in. He had taken me to Planned Parenthood, he had shushed my pleas to talk about it, he had groomed me for what he wanted; but in the end, he said he "could not make a silk purse out of a sow's ear." Depressed, devastated, and alone, I cried out in the middle of the night: "Oh, God … "

Shortly after the relationship ended, I decided to call my priest friend, Father Thomas, to whom I had not spoken for five years. His enthusiastic voice was cathartic, and I flew to Omaha for a visit. We went to a prayer meeting, and I was sensing the Holy Spirit's love through the Charismatic Renewal. I found purpose, returned to the Church, married, and had five children. Though outwardly we lived a Catholic life, I struggled internally with many things. The undertow of abuse, abortions, self-doubt, and shame still held me in anxiety and depression. I kept surfacing for air, but I could not live in peace.

Medication numbed me for years, and I believed if I could just make everything look perfect, then I would be acceptable. Before my fourth child was born, my water broke at nineteen weeks, and I was put on bed rest. For three and a half months, I lay in a quiet room on the second floor in order to retain whatever amniotic fluid remained. David was born at thirty-six weeks.

His under-developed lungs stopped working, and he died in my arms. There was tremendous grace in the room and in bringing him to the Sacrament of Baptism. I never felt punished by God for his death; in fact, I knew the Holy Spirit was imparting tremendous courage in the midst of overwhelming sorrow.

Grace was there, but grace does not make the imperfect appear to be perfect. Grace perfects the imperfect. A period of sanctification began.

The facade was crumbling. We had financial strain, our marriage suffered, and the combined issues of my husband's childhood and adolescent abuse and my own experiences began to surface in ways we did not know how to handle. There were many years of therapy and many prayers, but I did not encounter anyone with the knowledge and skills to deal with trauma.

Then, I found a new job with a Catholic radio station. I began receiving catechesis and exposure to Pope John Paul II. I started hearing about Theology of the Body, and my perceptions began to change. It was there I encountered Our Lady of Guadalupe, and I heard about Rachel's Vineyard Retreats. In 2005, I made my retreat and finally came to forgive myself. I was catapulted into an experience of grace that changed my life. Two years later, I attended Dr. Theresa Burke's leadership conference for Rachel's Vineyard and learned about her next retreat, from Grief to Grace — healing the wounds of abuse. My eyes were opened to the entanglement abuse played on my whole existence, and I began to process the trauma. The retreat revealed to me that I am a survivor, not a victim, and I can be immersed in Jesus, whose brutal suffering for love is my gateway to wholeness and holiness. With fervor, I returned to the sacraments. I was then moved to help pregnant women through a pro-life organization and went on to a life-coaching certification, using creative tools to help other abuse survivors find a path to healing in Christ.

A mature and unique Catholic therapist helped me process

my rage toward my father, stepfathers, and the sexual abuse of others. He helped me to see that though I admired my mother, she did not protect me, and I had to enter the "grief work" of what she exposed me to and of the years of my lost childhood.

Through another Catholic therapist, I experienced a healing of that horrible childhood scene of the knife at my mother's throat. Through her prayer of inviting the Holy Spirit into the memory, I saw Mary and Joseph standing with their hands clasped together around me, loving me and staying there until I was at peace. Then Mary dropped to her knees and scooped up my mother in her arms. Saint Joseph turned to my dad, who was still hovering with the knife, and touched his shoulder, and Dad's whole demeanor changed. This vision gives me hope as some of my children work through the effects of our brokenness that was passed to them.

Who am I today? On the outside, I look fairly normal. I still can experience triggers that make me doubt that I am acceptable or whole enough. Other times I struggle with anxiety and lack of confidence; but as these things come up, I recognize that I am in the rut of "freezing" my emotions, and then I allow myself to feel, to see what is going on, and to deal with it and let God heal it. I embrace Saint Ignatius's teaching on consolation, desolation, and the movements of the heart, believing that God is forming my soul, sometimes through the work of desolation. I make visits to the Eucharistic adoration chapel to just sit, to be loved and comforted, and to give back what is due to Jesus Christ, our redeeming Lord.

In 2011, my husband and I entered the Institute for Diaconate Formation. One of the basic requirements was that we be acquainted with suffering, so we knew we could fit right in. As training progressed, we were cemented in the love of God and came to understand that all along we contained seeds of greatness, and that our Lord was using our histories to bring about a greater goodness, brighter than any of the darkness. What had been forged in forty years of a committed marriage had healed and expanded my heart, and at my husband's ordination, I felt the exuberance of a bride, ready for the new journey.

God continues to make all things new. I have learned to love the beauty of my body, though now it is wrinkled and sagging. I can now appreciate the design of God — that men and women are made for each other, and that real intimacy was created by the Creator. It is beautiful. It is never for control or power or manipulation. Though my hope was deeply wounded, faith teaches me to rely on Jesus, who does not disappoint and has so much for me to discover. I search the horizon for another sweet soul who does not know her dignity and might need my love. What energizes me is gathering with others who match reciprocity with the empathy they receive in a cycle of restoration and hope.

Breaking the cycle of trauma. Inviting the cycle of restoration to take its place. Swords are made into plowshares. What was meant for evil, God redeems and makes new.

That is why I volunteer to serve on the Grief to Grace retreats. There, I witness the resurrection of other wounded souls. Through the many years of struggle, I would cling to this verse in Sacred Scripture: "The steadfast love of the Lord never ceases, his mercies never come to an end; they are new every morning; great is your faithfulness" (Lam 3:22–23).

PRAYER

Holy God,

Thank you for bringing moments of grace through service and opening Sacred Scripture to me. Those words of grace from Exodus 14:14 have given me hope so many times: "The Lord will fight for you, and you have only to be still."

Teach me to be still. Remind me that you are fighting for me and fill me with the confidence that with you as my sure defense, victory is certain.

Amen.

THE BODY HOLDS TRAUMA

"You heal, but the wounds never go away" (Kolk, 2014).

Jeannette and her siblings give us a very real example of how trauma is stored in the body. It shows us how this trauma can manifest as illness.

A survivor may mentally push trauma away, but it often stays in the body. The brain doesn't know how to react to trauma. It freezes. In that frozen state, the trauma gets stored. Our bodies store it as a defense mechanism to try to predict danger in the future, building a biological internal alarm system. However, as trauma accumulates and becomes more complex, those triggers and alarm systems have the potential to become faulty. They become hypervigilant and create constant states of fear and danger.

The memories may be repressed, but the body still feels. This disconnect causes intrusive feelings and emotions that seem to arise without a cause. The body doesn't know why it's feeling these things. It becomes very difficult for the survivor to answer questions about why they are having certain reactions. Trauma can create an emotional numbness to both emotions and physical sensations. As time passes, the sensations that the body is producing don't seem to have a logical cause-and-effect relationship. This causes extreme confusion and distress.

This means that you should avoid asking *why*. Questions like *Why do you feel this way?* or *Why did you do this?* are dead ends or worse. Such questions, referring to either the past or the present, just cause confusion and feelings of brokenness. The survivor doesn't know the answers. Not having answers that they are expected to have creates feelings of being crazy, broken, and unhealthy.

Getting away from the routines of everyday life and to a safe retreat and restoration space can be helpful in allowing the body to restore itself. Recommending a hiking trip or even a spiritual retreat outdoors can be helpful as well.

Because as we learn more about trauma and how it's stored in the body, we are finding somatic modalities of therapy very effective in treating trauma. It starts with the body.

DEACON MARTY'S STORY

I was born in Iowa, number five of six children. We grew up under conditions of strife and poverty. My father was an alcoholic who gambled, whose main interest was escaping into a bottle of wine. My mother, the oldest of two children, had been placed in an orphanage when she was eight years old, though both of her parents were still alive. Her brother was not put in the orphanage. Her father was an alcoholic and violently abused her. He had been forty-seven when he married her mother, who was just nineteen on the day of the wedding. My mother would have permanent physical reminders of the abuse she suffered at the hands of her father. I have never understood any of it. It is filed under the heading of "things people do that I will never understand," the first of many things I have had to put in that file throughout my life.

Orphanages in the early 1900s were the epitome of depravity. Because of her upbringing, my mother lacked the skills and experience to be a homemaker. She struggled with detachment issues and lacked the ability to nurture that seems to be a part of the feminine genius in most women. She also struggled with anger issues because of her father's abuse. She had difficulty expressing and giving love, even though she desired to be a mother.

The combination of my parents' issues created a tumultuous environment for us children growing up. I don't think there was a day that went by in which my parents didn't fight about something. The language they used was destructive, and the darkness cast a shadow over my siblings and me. My next older brother, Pat, was mentally handicapped, and when my parents would start fighting, he would begin sobbing and yelling at them to stop. My other siblings and I would attempt to calm him down and reassure him that everything would be okay, which wasn't the truth, but we were so upset to see him panic. If we could get him to calm down, then we could calm down. My siblings and I also suffered from extreme neglect. Although my father was a gentle-natured person when sober, we never felt safe. Looking back, I realize that my father must have been intoxicated all the time, yet I can't say that I ever saw him drunk. Still, the evidence was there; we would find empty bottles all around the house.

My family life caused deep problems of insecurity, fear, and low self-worth. My parents' constant fighting taught me to avoid conflict at any cost. I learned that disagreement and arguing never resolved anything and would always escalate into fighting. This traumatized me so much that I was unable to stand my ground in key moments of my life, because it seemed like I was already defeated.

The seeds of the evil one were planted to such a degree that it seemed my life meant nothing and would never amount to anything. I was not cherished. I was not lovable. I did not matter.

I felt isolated and alone. Nothing great here. It was a message I seemed to project. It was a reality I deeply felt. And yet, there was a whisper, a fleeting memory, telling me I was meant for greatness. Just as quickly, the thought would leave, and I would be left with the memories that suggested something else.

Despite my parents' problems, our Catholic faith was very important. One of my earliest memories was sitting at the kitchen table, looking at the pictures in our family Bible as my mother explained the stories to me. I had an experience where I felt a voice inside saying that I was created for greatness. I didn't know what that meant at the time, but those same words came back to me in my adult life. God wants to lift us up from the muddy clay and place us on solid ground (Ps 40:2). Throughout our lives, he whispers words of hope that come back to us, even in the midst of darkness.

We used to say the Rosary every evening after dinner. And my favorite memories are of being at church and gazing at the amazing stained-glass windows as the choir sang Christmas carols. I never wanted it to end. Moments of grace like that are sprinkled across my childhood.

We lived on the outskirts of town, but when I was seven, my parents lost the home we lived in. We moved in with an older woman and her blind brother until my parents were able to find a new home. I had never seen a blind man before, and I was amazed to see how he was able to do so many things despite his handicap. He could even play card games, and he was really a great card player! They were very kind to us, and I enjoyed the neighborhood we lived in during that time. I also realized that my parents were not fighting like they had been, probably because there were other adults around, and for a brief time I experienced peace. Then we moved into our new home in a different part of town. I was so excited! There were neighbors close to us, and my new school was two blocks away. I met one of the families that lived on our block, and I made my first friend. For a brief time. I was very happy.

It wasn't long after moving when, at the age of seven, I experienced the worst event of my life. Some of the older kids in the neighborhood were hanging out in the alley behind our house, and a couple of my friends and I joined them to see what they were up to. They took me into a nearby garage and raped me. I had no idea what was happening, and they demanded that I do exactly what they said, or they would beat me up. It was terrifying. They were much bigger, and my own friends couldn't do anything to stop them. All I remember was feeling pain and humiliation. Why? How could they do this? I was so confused. Everything else was just a blur. I don't remember words spoken or seeing their faces.

From that moment on, I never felt that I was anyone's equal. I became a target of abusive behaviors, almost like I was a piñata for other kids to beat on. Would I have to put up with this sort of thing just to be with other kids? I developed serious nervous habits. I started experiencing tremors in my hands, which I still have to this day, although not as severe as they were back then.

I was always sizing up my surroundings when I was in a group of other boys, wondering which one was going to be my next abuser. I was a very gentle person, and I never treated others with disrespect or mistreatment. Yet there I was, taking on all the abuse, name-calling, taunting, and teasing, mainly because they knew that I wouldn't fight back. I didn't know how they knew — they just knew.

In the wild, the wounded animal becomes the target. The weak one is marked. Yet God did not create human beings for this. He placed within us an eternal soul, but evil seeks to make us into animals, to thrust us into a world of predator and prey. I felt the label: "Prey." I longed for a rightly ordered world in which I could know what God knows when he looks at me: That

I was made for greatness.

My mother saw how I was being treated by other kids, and she became very angry with my father, because he did nothing to teach me how to fight back. My father was a passive man who walked away from conflict, even when his own son needed him to intervene. Even if he couldn't teach me to fight back against my abusers, I wanted my father to be with me and to spend time doing things with him. I wanted to feel safe, to feel loved, to feel protected, but his own demons prevented him from spending one-on-one time with me. A father's love and attentiveness can mitigate even the most horrific experiences. A paternal void can exacerbate the same.

RECOGNIZING SIGNS

Before listing signs of sexual abuse, it is very important to note that you shouldn't jump to conclusions. Seeing one or even multiple signs from the list below doesn't necessarily mean that sexual abuse is happening. It means that it *might* be happening. Be careful not to jump to conclusions. Be careful not to make assumptions. Be careful not to judge or gossip.

Many of these signs could also indicate something else entirely. It is damaging to the individual and community to prematurely accuse someone of abuse prior to its confirmation.

Signs of sexual abuse include the following, but are not limited to:

- hypersexualization or knowledge of adult issues not appropriate to their age
- isolation/becoming withdrawn; a lack of desire to spend time with certain people

or visit certain places
- adults wanting to be alone with children
- anxiety and immobilization, freeze responses
- states of being fearful
- signs of physical markings or bruises
- sudden changes in behavior (a coworker abruptly deciding to stop going out, a friend becoming withdrawn, a family member not wanting stay in a hotel alone or not wanting to talk with a specific person)
- sudden changes in personality
- becoming uncharacteristically aggressive
- lack of social skills and having very few friends
- poor bond or relationship with parent
- running away
- self-harm
- wanting to hide themselves physically or with clothing

These signs are reasons to be curious in gentle ways. Don't assume you know what's happening or make accusations. Open conversations and respect boundaries. Remember that these signs may mean sexual abuse is/has occurred, but they could also have many other meanings or causes. Remain curious and mindful.

If someone tells you they have experienced abuse, it's important to believe them. Do not question them or indicate that you have doubts. Remember that one of the main reasons survivors don't share is the fear of not being believed. In the moment of someone sharing, believe them.

As I got a little older, I realized that our neighborhood was not in the better part of town. Most of my friends came from blue-collar families, and they experienced a lot of abuse and alcohol-related problems and domestic violence, much of it even worse than that in my family. My mother told me that she hated moving into this neighborhood, but it was all they could afford at the time.

I was filled with rage toward my abusers, but I didn't have it in me to do anything about it. I would sometimes dream of ways to get back at them, but once I had any thoughts of violence toward them, I would shut the thoughts down. Instead, I coped with the effects of my abuse by doing things on my own, away from my friends and the unsavory environment in the neighborhood. I started exploring, taking walks, primarily by following the railroad tracks that went right by our house. Eventually, I would end up by the river that ran through the center of town. This became my escape from the rest of the world.

I loved nature and found all sorts of things to do near the river. I would catch huge bullfrogs that lived along the water's edge. I discovered crayfish in the shallow pools along the riverbank and fish that would come into the shallows. I learned to skip rocks and find gooseberries. Occasionally I came across a fisherman. I found peace there, and it gave me the opportunity to discover beauty, something sorely missing at home. I stumbled upon one of my first passions as well: fishing. I became intrigued as I observed anglers practicing their craft, noticing the different techniques for casting and retrieving and, most importantly, watching them catch these fascinating creatures. I was hooked! I also found out that it was something my father loved to do, too. At last, I thought, here was something that I could convince my father to do with me. I must have driven him crazy as a result. We did do some fishing together, but eventually, like everything else, that stopped. I lived in the promise that he would take me fishing. He even said that we would go to Minnesota — where real fishermen went — on a fishing trip, but that day never came.

When I was about ten, I met the girl who would eventually become my wife, Jeanette Dilley. She was dating my older brother Tim. They were four years ahead of me in school, and I thought that she was the nicest person I had ever met, and so pretty. I thought my brother was the luckiest guy in the world, and our family always enjoyed when she would come to the house to visit.

When I was about eleven, the older brother of one of my classmates showed up in the neighborhood. We had attended the same school before my family moved, and he began to seek me out. I didn't think it was odd that he wanted to hang out with someone four years younger than he was. I had no strong father figure, and I was simply glad that an older man wanted to hang out with me.

As we roamed the neighborhood, we passed by a parking lot adjacent to a packing plant that was a couple blocks away from my house. I showed him an old bread delivery truck that had been left at one end of the lot. My friends and I would often hang out in it, pretending we were driving it and making up stories of racing, chasing other vehicles, and so on. He and I were in the back of the truck when he approached me from behind and started forcefully pulling my pants down. Instead of freezing, I yelled at him to stop. I don't remember what I said, but it must have scared him enough, because he backed away.

I was not frightened this time, as I had been when I was seven, but I was confused about why boys wanted to have sex with me. What was wrong with me, that I was attracting this behavior? I thought I was the problem. I didn't realize that I was simply there, young, vulnerable, easily overcome. I still did not understand that these incidents were rape. Back then, I thought rape was only what some depraved men did to women. And didn't boys like girls? I knew nothing about homosexuality or same-sex attraction. I didn't have a language for any of it. I was confused, living in shame, and there was no way that I could ever tell my parents about my experiences. I was so afraid that I would be punished for what happened. I couldn't talk with my buddies either, so everything got pushed down.

Once I entered adolescence, I grew to be the biggest kid in my grade. I never saw myself that way. I was the gentle soul who was still afraid of fighting and lacked the confidence to stand up for himself. Now that I was bigger, I often found myself the target of older kids who picked me out of the crowd because of my size. They were always older, smaller, and often intoxicated. There was only one time that I ever won a fight. It was when a kid started beating up my brother Pat, who was mentally handicapped. I didn't hold back. That bully was eating dirt by the time I finished with him. I hated fighting, winning or losing, but from that day on, everyone left my brother alone.

As I went through high school, I found new friends and activities that I really enjoyed. I played sports, mainly football, basketball, and track and field. I loved music, and I sang in the choir. I also developed a passion for science and biology. Unfortunately, I still struggled with bullying, and it was much worse in high school. I didn't know what was going on with me then, but I started suffering from depression. Once, I missed sixteen consecutive days of school because I just couldn't get out of bed and face the abuse. I kept telling my parents I didn't feel well, but I couldn't let them know what was really going on. I went to the doctor for a check-up, and he found nothing wrong with me. My older siblings badgered me to get up and go to school. I felt like a liar, because physically there was nothing wrong with me. I also felt like such a loser, thinking it was all my fault, not realizing psychologically what was going on. Eventually, I did return to school.

The rage inside me finally started to find its way to the surface when, one day after football practice, I was in the shower. One of my tormentors had taken a bar of soap and threw it at me. I grabbed it and threw it back at him with every ounce of my strength. It just missed his head and completely shattered as it hit the wall. We immediately charged at each other, but the rest of the teammates stopped us. We started yelling and swearing at each other, saying this wasn't over. We never did take further steps to finish our confrontation, but that day, the abuse stopped.

My confidence continued to suffer, however. I realized this after I started dating my first girlfriend. My past had caused me to shut down my feelings, and this was painfully evident in my inability to express my true affections in the relationship. I couldn't talk or show the kind of tenderness that I felt for her and that she deserved. It didn't take long for her to break off the relationship. I felt devastated, and it took a long time to get over it. I would have similar problems in future relationships.

When I was in my later teens, my parents started getting counseling. They met regularly with a priest, who eventually became a close family friend. My mother told me about what a wonderful man he was. She felt quite comfortable with him because of the counseling. He started coming over to our house for visits and meals. He was a talented musician himself and showed a lot of interest in my being in choir and loving music. He encouraged me to pursue music.

At some point, though, I became aware that this priest had some serious personal issues. For one thing, he was an alcoholic, and sometimes he came to our house intoxicated. On those occasions, his behavior was quite different, and he took an increased interest in me, which made me extremely uneasy. He also confessed to me that he had same-sex attractions. I felt that this disclosure was inappropriate, and I did not want to be around him from that point on. My mother told me not to judge him and that it was wrong to reject him due to his personal struggles. As difficult as it was for me to be in his presence, I attempted to follow her advice and practice charity toward him; it took every ounce of courage I had.

One evening, he showed up very intoxicated and in no condition to drive home, so my parents invited him to stay at our place. My mother decided to put him in my room, as it was the only room with an extra bed. That night, he talked to me for what seemed like hours, sharing how miserable his life was. He told me that, had he been married, he would have loved to have a son just like me. Then he placed his hand on me in a way that gave me the creeps. My mother had unknowingly enabled the situation, but I would never be able to bring myself to tell her about this. I couldn't get her words about not judging him out of my head. I felt trapped. I was afraid and angry at the same time. I wanted to hit him, yet all I could think was, "He's a priest! I can't treat him like that! What the hell am I going to do?" At some point, he stopped and apologized for his behavior. Somehow, I got through that night and was relieved when morning came and I could get as far from him as possible.

After that, I stopped going to Mass and wanted nothing to do with church. I even questioned the existence of God and refused any invitation or challenge to participate in anything church-related.

When I finished high school, I went to work in construction for a while, mostly out of town. It got me away from the people who were trying to get me back to the Faith, but it didn't get me away from my problems. I felt lost, with no meaning or purpose in my life. Even though I was being a responsible person, I felt so empty.

That all began to change when Jeanette moved back to town from New York. She reconnected with my family. I was so happy to see her. She had a huge impact on my family by getting my brother and me to start going back to church. I experienced a deep conversion that revitalized my faith. I had fallen in love with Jesus Christ! Jeanette and I began participating in the music at our parish, and we became good friends. That friendship led to dating, and eventually we married. We had five children and a full life, but the wounds of the past began to show up in our relationship. It was still difficult for me to talk about my feelings, and I failed to express my affection for my wife adequately and ensure growth in marital communication and intimacy. I loved my wife very much, but I lacked the ability to show how much I really cared for her and for our family. My relationship with our children became difficult as well, especially as they grew into adolescence. I lacked confidence as a husband and father. We went to counseling, both individually and as a couple. We both wanted our life to work, and our faith kept us strong through the difficult years. Even though therapy was very helpful, there was still something blocking my sense of well-being. I suffered from shame, guilt, and unworthiness, but I couldn't understand why.

I had never talked to anyone about my abuse. Finally, I shared with my wife, and I began to see that abuse was at the root of my dark feelings. I had distanced myself from those memories and did not realize the impact they had on my life. In prayer and reflection, I finally came to the spiritual understanding that I needed to unite my sufferings with those of Jesus on the cross. I didn't have to bear these things on my own. He completely understood what I had been through for so long. The final healing would occur while attending a Grief to Grace Retreat for trauma and abuse in 2008. This retreat gave me the knowledge, understanding, and grace to be vulnerable enough to express those feelings that had been buried. I finally let go of the sorrow, anger, abandonment, self-loathing, shame, and guilt. None of it was my fault, and for the first time, I knew this was true.

In 1997, while singing in the church choir, I had sensed a call to become a deacon. I did not move ahead with it until after I received the healing through the Grief to Grace retreat. I finally entered formation in 2010 and was ordained in 2015. Part of my passion in ministry is to work with survivors of trauma and abuse. My formation, life experience, and healing have uniquely qualified me to enter this life-affirming work.

Through all of this, my relationship with my wife has changed dramatically. My relationship with my children continues to grow, and our life is much fuller. Just as music was our first combined expression of service and love for Jesus Christ, now my wife and I work in unison to bring healing and wholeness to those who have been abused.

PRAYER

Lord Jesus Christ,

I know that I was not made for self-loathing and shame. I was made for greatness. I give you thanks and praise for the plan you had in mind for me, a plan to lift me out of the miry clay and place my feet on solid ground. A plan to raise me up, heal me, and direct me to go out and help others.

Continue to guide me in this ministry of healing. Use me, Lord, so that others may know wholeness as they, too, are lifted from the miry clay and discover the greatness you have waiting for them.

Amen.

VICARIOUS TRAUMA AND REASONS TO LOOK OUT FOR IT

The brain has a vivid imagination. If we are not firmly grounded in the present moment, our brain cannot distinguish between *now* and *then*. When we hear stories in graphic detail, our imagination can start to go wild, if we let it. The brain does not distinguish between the event happening to someone else at another time and what is or is not happening in the here and now. It's similar to a nightmare in which you are falling, and when you wake up, your body is acting as if those events were really occurring, though it was just happening in your mind. The body may be sweaty, shaky, with a racing heart, or frozen. If you are mindful when watching a thriller, you may notice your heart racing, sweaty palms, etc. This is because the mind actually believes it's happening, even though part of you knows it's fiction.

If you are someone who hears stories often, it can cause buildup of somatic symptoms in the body. You may find yourself becoming more irritable, unable to sleep, having more nightmares, more tension in the body, more headaches, and other symptoms. This is also true if you are taking in a lot of news, or if you drive by a car accident, or take in photos of trauma. It's important to be aware of how much traumatic material you are taking in, in your everyday life.

It's important to be mindful of your own emotional and physical reactions when listening and being present to another's story. This can get in the way of you offering a grounded, calming, predictable, and reliable place for them to come to. It's also important to have your own list of ways to self-care as you minister. This will help you release some of what you may take in and prevent burnout in a serving profession.

Some ideas include:

- taking walks
- talking with someone
- prayer/mindfulness
- drinking water
- exercise
- getting a hug
- doing your own grounding exercises

HOPE FOR HEALING

The information included in this book is a glimpse into the knowledge, research, and resources that exist for helping sexual abuse survivors. Please rely on more than just the information in this book. Do your own reading and research, as well.

Every day, we learn more about trauma. Every day, there are advances in neuroscience. We are constantly developing more and more effective modalities to help those who have been sexually abused.

There is hope, and there is a way to escape.

The following is a list of resources to get you started. These resources are meant for both the survivor and for those who happen to be in a position to help.

RETREATS

Grief to Grace (for healing of abuse): http://grief-to-grace-lsi.squarespace.com

Rachel's Vineyard (for post-abortive healing): https://www.rachelsvineyard.org

GENERAL RESOURCES

National Sexual Assault Hotline: Call 800-656-HOPE (4673) to be connected with a trained staff member from a sexual assault service provider in your area.

National Child Traumatic Stress Network (NCTSN): Effective treatments for youth, trauma training, and education measures; reviews of measures examining trauma for parents, educators, judges, child welfare agencies, military personnel, and therapists, https://www.nctsn.org/

RISE Catholic network of resources for those who experienced sexual assault from the Archdiocese of Denver: https://www.riseaod.org

RISE network of resources for sexual assault victims: https://www.riseslo.org/sexual_assault_abuse_survivors.php

Gift from Within PTSD resources for survivors and caregivers: https://www.giftfromwithin.org

Office for Victims of Crime in the Department of Justice: Provides resources for a variety of victims and has a National Directory of Victim assistance funding opportunities, http://ojp.gov/ovc/.

FIND A THERAPIST

HelpPRO Therapist Finder: Comprehensive listing of local therapists specializing in trauma and other concerns, serving specific age groups, http://www.helppro.com/

Find a Catholic therapist near you: https://www.catholictherapists.com

Find a therapist and information on somatic and trauma-based treatment approaches:

- Brainspotting: https://brainspotting.com
- EMDR: http://www.emdria.org/
- Somatic Experiencing: https://traumahealing.org
- Internal Family Systems therapy: https://ifs-institute.com

To report any sexual abuse within your diocese, contact your local Victim Assistance Coordinator, which you can find at the following link: https://www.usccb.org/offices/child-and-youth-protection/victim-assistance

ABOUT THE CONTRIBUTORS

Lisa Mladinich is a Catholic wife and mom, author, speaker, life coach, and host for Shalom World TV. She speaks and leads retreats across the country.

Denise Bossert is a mother and grandmother. She has taught theology and is an author, editor, and Catholic speaker.

Courtney Hempstead is a single mother and pre-law student. She is a convert to the Catholic Church.

Patty Capetillo works as a pediatric nurse practitioner in Texas. She is the mother of two daughters and a lifelong Catholic. She is active in ACTS Retreats, a ministry instrumental in her journey to healing and wholeness.

Marguerite Ogden is a doctor of audiology, living with her husband and three children in Houston, Texas.

Deacon Marty and **Jeanette Meyer** live in Minnesota and have dedicated their lives to helping survivors of assault. They facilitate Grief to Grace Retreats in North America.

For Further Reading

GLIMMERS OF GRACE

Moments of Peace and Healing Following Sexual Abuse

[illegible] with [illegible] Ball

The day that 18-year-old Faith Hakesley was to testify in court against the well-liked Catholic priest who had raped her, a court guard pressed [illegible] in her hand. It was the first glimmer.

The little piece of candy reminded her of the Scripture about faith the size of a mustard seed, and this bit of encouragement, by way of the guard, but really from God, gave her the courage she needed to endure the trial.

In *Glimmers of Grace: Moments of Peace and Healing Following Sexual Abuse*, Faith shares what she has learned about the gifts God wants to give victims throughout their journey of healing. Each personal and [illegible] glimmer of grace [illegible] to see them as a pathway to true freedom.

[illegible] reflection [illegible] explores [illegible] including:

- [illegible]
- Kindness
- [illegible]
- Self-compassion

Each reflection includes [illegible] and journaling questions to help [illegible] Faith [illegible] and how God is speaking to you and find hope and healing after sexual abuse.

OSV[illegible]CatholicBookStore.com
or wherever books are sold.